Introduction: Navigating Love and Celebrations in Authenticity

Welcome to the enchanting journey of wedding planning, where love takes center stage and authenticity is the guiding star. In the vast landscape of weddings, every couple's tale is a unique masterpiece, a narrative woven from the threads of their shared dreams and individual identities. As we embark on this adventure, this inclusive wedding planning guide is crafted with one clear mission in mind: to empower and celebrate trans couples navigating the joyous path toward their special day.

Love is a remarkable force, transcending boundaries and societal norms. Yet, planning a wedding can sometimes feel like a labyrinth, especially when your journey as a trans individual adds a layer of complexity to the process. This guide is here to serve as your compass, ensuring that every step you take is a stride toward an authentic and meaningful celebration of your love.

Chapter by chapter, we will delve into the intricacies of wedding planning through the lens of inclusivity, respect, and understanding. From defining your unique vision to selecting the perfect attire that aligns with your true selves, each section is designed to empower you in making choices that resonate with your authentic identity.

Navigating family dynamics can be both heartwarming and challenging. Communication is key, and we'll explore tips on how to approach conversations with grace, involving your loved ones in the planning process. As we move forward, we'll guide you in assembling your dream team of trans-friendly vendors, ensuring your wedding day is surrounded by supportive professionals who share your vision.

Ceremonies and rituals hold a special place in our hearts, and we'll explore how to create a ceremony that is not only trans-inclusive but also filled with deep, personal meaning. Legalities and documentation can be daunting, but fear not; we'll break down the essentials, making sure you are well-prepared for this aspect of the journey.

Whether you're considering a honeymoon getaway, navigating parenthood, or taking the DIY route, this guide is your trusted companion. Let's embark on this transformative journey together, celebrating love in all its authenticity, diversity, and beauty. Your wedding day is a canvas waiting to be painted with the hues of your unique love story, and we're here to help you create a masterpiece that will be cherished for a lifetime.

Chapter 1: Understanding Your Vision

Welcome to the exhilarating world of wedding planning, where dreams take shape and love is celebrated in all its splendor. In Chapter 1: Understanding Your Vision, we embark on a journey of self-discovery and creative exploration, laying the foundation for a wedding that is uniquely and authentically yours.

Your wedding is not just an event; it's a reflection of your love story, a day woven with the threads of your shared experiences and individual identities. Understanding Your Vision is the cornerstone of a wedding that resonates with your authenticity, capturing the essence of who you are as a couple.

As you dive into this chapter, consider it a guided meditation on the aspirations you hold for your special day. We'll explore ways to define and articulate your unique wedding narrative, uncovering the elements that make your love story extraordinary. What traditions resonate with you? How can you infuse cultural or personal nuances into your celebration? These are the questions we'll unravel together, empowering you to craft a vision that feels genuine and true.

Authenticity is the heartbeat of a trans-inclusive wedding, and this chapter serves as your compass in navigating the vast landscape of possibilities. Embrace the joy of envisioning a celebration that not only aligns with your values but also radiates the love you share with your partner.

Setting the stage for inclusivity, we'll discuss the importance of establishing goals that reflect your commitment to creating a wedding environment where all feel welcome and appreciated. This chapter isn't just about planning; it's about creating a space for love to thrive, unencumbered by societal expectations or constraints.

So, let's embark on this delightful exploration together, where your imagination takes flight, and your wedding vision begins to crystallize. By the end of this chapter, you'll not only have a clearer picture of your dream wedding but also a roadmap for infusing it with the authenticity that will make it truly unforgettable. Here's to discovering the magic of your vision and setting the stage for a celebration as unique and extraordinary as your love.

Defining Your Unique Wedding Narrative

Welcome to the exhilarating journey of defining your unique wedding narrative—a journey that encapsulates the very essence of your love story and sets the stage for a celebration as distinctive as your partnership. In this section, we dive into the art of self-reflection and storytelling, laying the groundwork for a wedding that mirrors the authentic beauty of your relationship.

Your love story is a tapestry of shared moments, challenges overcome, and the joyous milestones that have brought you to this moment of planning your wedding. As you embark on this section, envision it as a heartfelt conversation with your partner, an exploration of the threads that weave your narrative together.

Begin by reflecting on the pivotal moments of your relationship. What brought you two together? How did you navigate challenges and celebrate triumphs as a couple? Consider the shared interests, passions, and values that define your connection. These elements will serve as the palette from which you'll draw inspiration to paint the picture of your wedding narrative.

Now, let's delve into the unique aspects of your journey. Perhaps your love story is a testament to resilience, overcoming obstacles with unwavering determination. Or, it might be a tale of serendipity, where unexpected encounters shaped the course of your shared destiny. Take a moment to articulate the qualities that make your narrative extraordinary and distinctly yours.

As you define your unique wedding narrative, consider the cultural and familial influences that have shaped your identities. How do you want to honor and incorporate these aspects into your celebration? Whether it's a nod to cultural traditions, a fusion of diverse backgrounds, or a celebration of chosen family, let your narrative be a canvas that embraces the richness of your experiences.

Think about the values that anchor your relationship. Is it a commitment to equality, authenticity, or adventure? Your wedding narrative is an opportunity to infuse these values into every aspect of your celebration, creating a cohesive and meaningful experience for both you and your guests.

In crafting your narrative, explore the roles of each partner. How do your individual stories converge into a shared chapter? Celebrate the unique qualities that each of you brings to the relationship, acknowledging the strengths that complement one another. Your wedding is a collaborative masterpiece, a reflection of the beautiful synergy that defines your partnership.

This section is more than a step in the wedding planning process; it's a chance to embark on a journey of self-discovery as a couple. By defining your unique wedding narrative, you set the stage for a celebration that not only mirrors your love but also invites others to witness and share in the magic of your story. As you navigate this exploration, remember that your narrative is a living, breathing entity—allow it to evolve and unfold organically, just as your love story continues to do.

Embracing Authenticity: Reflecting Your True Selves

In this vibrant section, we embark on a journey to embrace authenticity—a journey that transcends the traditional confines of wedding planning and encourages you to reflect your true selves in every facet of your celebration. Your wedding is a canvas where your authentic selves can shine, and this chapter is all about giving yourself the freedom to express, celebrate, and amplify the uniqueness that defines you as a couple.

Authenticity is a powerful force that transforms a wedding from a mere event into a soul-stirring experience. It's about casting aside societal expectations and embracing your genuine identity as a couple. As you delve into this exploration, consider it a celebration of the beautiful tapestry that is your love story—one that deserves to be told authentically and unapologetically.

Start by reflecting on your personal styles and tastes. What makes you feel comfortable, confident, and true to yourselves? Whether it's a vintage-inspired gown, a tailored suit, or a fusion of cultural attire, your wedding attire is a tangible expression of your authentic selves. Allow your fashion choices to reflect the unique personalities that come together in your relationship.

Beyond attire, think about the overall ambiance you want to create. How can you infuse your personalities into the details of your celebration? From décor to music, each element offers an opportunity to showcase the facets of your identities. Whether it's incorporating shared hobbies, favorite colors, or significant symbols, let these details tell a story that is distinctly yours.

Consider how you want to express your gender identity during the celebration. This might involve reimagining traditional roles within the wedding party, opting for gender-neutral language in your ceremony, or embracing non-binary expressions. Your wedding is a space to honor and celebrate the authenticity of your gender identities, creating an environment that feels genuine and affirming.

Moreover, authenticity extends to the very essence of your relationship. Your love is unique, and your wedding should reflect that. Whether you've been together for years or a short while, your journey is significant and deserving of celebration. Share the quirks, inside jokes, and moments that define your partnership. Your guests will appreciate the sincerity and intimacy that comes from embracing your relationship's authentic narrative.

This chapter invites you to challenge preconceived notions and expectations. It encourages you to forge a path that is true to your vision rather than adhering to societal norms. In doing so, you create a wedding that is not only visually stunning but emotionally resonant—a celebration that captures the true essence of your love.

As you navigate the process of embracing authenticity, remember that this is a journey of self-discovery and self-expression. It's about creating a wedding that feels like a natural extension of who you are as individuals and as a couple. By infusing authenticity into every aspect of your celebration, you ensure that your wedding is not just an event but a genuine reflection of the love that binds you together.

Setting Inclusive Goals for Your Special Day

As we continue our journey through the delightful expanse of wedding planning, we now delve into the enriching process of setting inclusive goals for your special day. Your wedding is not just a celebration of love between you and your partner; it's an opportunity to create an atmosphere of warmth and acceptance for everyone involved. This chapter invites you to envision a celebration that reflects the principles of inclusivity, ensuring that every guest feels valued and welcomed.

Start by considering the atmosphere you want to cultivate. How can you create a space that feels inviting and affirming for all your guests? Setting inclusive goals involves recognizing the diversity within your guest list and taking steps to honor and celebrate that diversity. This might involve incorporating inclusive language in your ceremony, providing accessible seating options, or ensuring that your chosen venue is welcoming to everyone.

Think about the traditions and rituals you want to include in your celebration. How can you adapt or create customs that resonate with a diverse audience? Setting inclusive goals means actively considering the experiences of all your guests, ensuring that your wedding is a space where everyone can participate and feel a sense of belonging.

Consider the importance of representation. Are there ways to showcase diversity in your wedding party, ceremony, or décor? By setting goals that prioritize representation, you contribute to a more inclusive narrative that reflects the richness of human experience. This might involve selecting a diverse group of vendors, including LGBTQ+ and BIPOC representation in your wedding party, or incorporating cultural elements that celebrate different heritages.

Inclusivity also extends to the little details that can make a significant impact. From dietary considerations to language choices, every decision you make contributes to the overall inclusivity of your celebration. Setting goals to accommodate various needs ensures that your guests feel seen and valued.

Think about the accessibility of your wedding venue. Are there accommodations that can be made to ensure that everyone, regardless of mobility, feels comfortable and included? Whether it's providing ramps, accessible restrooms, or sign language interpreters, setting inclusive goals involves considering the diverse needs of your guests and taking proactive steps to meet those needs.

As you set inclusive goals for your special day, involve your partner in the conversation. This is a collaborative effort that reflects the shared values of your relationship. Discuss what inclusivity means to both of you and how you can collectively work towards creating a celebration that aligns with those values.

Remember, setting inclusive goals is an ongoing process that evolves as your plans take shape. It involves a commitment to learning, adapting, and actively seeking ways to make your wedding a celebration that resonates with everyone present. By approaching this chapter with an open heart and a dedication to inclusivity, you contribute to a wedding experience that goes beyond the ordinary, creating a space where love and acceptance flourish.

Overcoming Stereotypes: Redefining Wedding Traditions

In the enchanting realm of wedding planning, there often exists a trove of traditions, each with its own set of expectations and norms. Yet, in this section, we embark on a liberating journey of overcoming stereotypes, challenging preconceived notions, and redefining wedding traditions to better align with the authenticity of your love story.

Traditions, while steeped in history and cultural significance, can sometimes feel restrictive. They may carry gendered expectations or assumptions that don't resonate with the diverse identities and relationships of today. As you navigate this section, consider it an invitation to reassess these traditions and, when necessary, reimagine them in a way that speaks to the unique essence of your partnership.

Start by reflecting on the typical gender roles assigned in weddings. Are there elements that feel restrictive or misaligned with your relationship? This is an opportunity to break free from stereotypical expectations and craft roles within your wedding party and ceremony that reflect the equality and authenticity you value.

Consider the wedding attire—often laden with gender-specific expectations. How can you redefine traditional attire choices to authentically express your identities? Whether it's experimenting with colors, styles, or accessories, this is a chance to transcend the conventional and embrace attire that feels genuinely reflective of who you are.

Wedding ceremonies, too, carry their own set of expectations. From the processional to the exchange of vows, traditions may not always align with the diversity of relationships and experiences. Challenge these norms by considering alternatives or modifications that better suit your vision. This might involve creating non-traditional vows, crafting a unique processional, or incorporating rituals that are personally meaningful.

The language used in ceremonies and announcements is another area ripe for transformation. Wedding scripts often default to heteronormative and binary language. By redefining the language used in your ceremony, you not only ensure that it resonates with your relationship but also create a space that is inclusive for all attendees, regardless of their identities.

Think about wedding party roles and expectations. Do away with assumptions about who should fulfill specific roles based on gender or relationships. Embrace a diverse and inclusive wedding party that represents the meaningful connections in your life, regardless of societal norms.

This journey of overcoming stereotypes is not about discarding tradition entirely but rather about reassessing and embracing what feels authentic to you. It's about recognizing that your love story is unique, and your wedding should be a reflection of that uniqueness. As you redefine wedding traditions, you contribute to a broader shift in the narrative, creating a space where love is celebrated in all its forms.

Approach this piece with an open heart and a willingness to challenge norms. Embrace the opportunity to pave the way for a wedding that defies stereotypes and honors the authenticity of your relationship. By doing so, you not only create a celebration that feels true to you but also contribute to a more inclusive and accepting landscape for future couples to come.

Creating a Trans-Inclusive Wedding Vision Board

In the whimsical realm of wedding planning, where dreams and creativity converge, we now venture into the delightful process of creating a trans-inclusive wedding vision board. Think of this as a hands-on, visual journey that transcends the ordinary and allows you to craft a vivid representation of the love story you're ready to celebrate.

A vision board is not just a collage of pretty pictures; it's a powerful tool that helps you clarify, concentrate, and maintain focus on your goals. In the context of a trans-inclusive wedding, it becomes a canvas where you can weave together the elements that matter most to you and your partner.

Begin this creative endeavor by gathering materials that spark joy and inspiration. Magazines, photographs, fabric swatches, and even digital images can all find a place on your vision board. This isn't just about aesthetics; it's about curating a collection of visuals that resonate with the authentic narrative of your love story.

Consider the theme and mood you want your wedding to embody. Is it whimsical and playful? Elegant and sophisticated? By selecting images that capture the essence of your vision, you begin to shape the overall atmosphere you wish to create. Let your instincts guide you, allowing your vision board to be a reflection of the emotions you hope to evoke on your special day.

As a trans couple, your wedding vision board holds the power to redefine traditional norms and showcase the beauty of gender diversity. Explore images that reflect your desired attire, from gender-affirming wedding gowns to tailored suits that align with your identities. Let the colors, textures, and styles convey the uniqueness of your love story.

Inclusivity should be a central theme on your vision board. Seek out images that represent a diverse range of relationships, gender expressions, and cultural influences. Let this visual representation remind you that your wedding is a celebration of love that transcends boundaries and embraces the rich tapestry of human experiences.

Don't shy away from incorporating symbols and elements that hold personal significance. Whether it's incorporating LGBTQ+ pride colors, cultural symbols, or representations of chosen family, each image should tell a story that goes beyond the surface and reflects the layers of your relationship.

Consider the venue and setting of your dreams. Whether it's an intimate garden ceremony, a beachfront celebration, or an elegant ballroom affair, find images that resonate with your ideal backdrop. Let these visuals transport you to the atmosphere you envision for your wedding day.

As you arrange your vision board, embrace the fluidity and creativity of the process. There are no rules; it's about allowing your imagination to guide you. Your vision board is a living, evolving entity, much like your love story. Feel free to add, subtract, and refine as your wedding plans unfold and your vision becomes clearer.

This creative journey is not just about the final product; it's about the process of discovery and self-expression. Your trans-inclusive wedding vision board is a testament to the unique narrative you're crafting—a celebration that is authentically and unapologetically yours. So, gather your materials, let your creativity flow, and watch as your vision board becomes a visual manifestation of the love story you're ready to share with the world.

Chapter 2: Attire and Expression

Welcome to the enchanting world of Chapter 2: Attire and Expression, where we embark on a delightful exploration of the threads that weave your love story into the very fabric of your wedding day. In this chapter, we delve into the art of self-expression through attire, celebrating the beauty of diverse identities and paving the way for a wardrobe that authentically reflects who you are as a couple.

Your wedding attire is not just clothing; it's a statement, a visual manifestation of your unique love story. As you navigate this chapter, envision it as a journey through a vibrant spectrum of possibilities, where the conventional boundaries of bridal and groom wear melt away, making room for a celebration of authenticity and self-expression.

Let's begin with the concept of attire as a means of storytelling. Each garment, each accessory, holds the potential to convey the nuances of your relationship. Whether you're leaning toward timeless classics, contemporary styles, or a fusion of cultural elements, your wedding attire becomes a canvas for expressing your shared vision and individual identities.

Consider the traditional norms that often accompany wedding attire and how they might intersect with your identities. This chapter is an invitation to challenge those norms, to embrace the freedom of choice, and to redefine what wedding attire means for you. From bridal gowns to groom suits, the possibilities are boundless, and the choices are yours to make.

Beyond the aesthetics, we'll explore the significance of comfort and confidence in your chosen attire. Your wedding day is a celebration, a momentous occasion where you should feel entirely at ease. We'll navigate the realm of fabrics, styles, and accessories, ensuring that your attire not only looks stunning but also aligns with the comfort that allows you to fully embrace the joy of the day.

In the spirit of inclusivity, we'll delve into attire choices that celebrate gender diversity. Whether you're navigating the aisle in a gown, a suit, or a blend of both, your wedding attire is an opportunity to redefine gender norms and showcase the authentic expressions of your love. We'll explore gender-affirming options and tips for creating a wardrobe that feels true to your identity.

This chapter invites you to not only choose attire but to curate a visual symphony that resonates with your love story. It's about embracing the art of self-expression, transcending societal expectations, and crafting a visual narrative that feels genuine and resonant. So, let the journey through Chapter 2 unfold, and may your wedding attire be a testament to the beauty of diversity and the authenticity that defines your remarkable love.

Navigating Fashion Choices: Bridal, Groom, and Beyond

In the vibrant tapestry of wedding planning, one of the most exciting and expressive chapters unfolds as we navigate the world of fashion choices—bridal, groom, and beyond. This is not merely about selecting garments; it's a journey through the myriad possibilities of self-expression, a celebration of individuality, and an exploration of the diverse threads that weave your love story.

For brides, the conventional image of a flowing white gown may come to mind, but the realm of bridal fashion is anything but limited. Today's brides are embracing a spectrum of styles, from elegant ball gowns to sleek pantsuits, whimsical tea-length dresses to cultural attire that pays homage to diverse heritages. The key lies in allowing your personal style and vision to guide you, creating a bridal look that not only resonates with your identity but also aligns with the atmosphere you wish to evoke on your wedding day.

Grooms, too, are breaking free from traditional molds and embracing fashion choices that mirror their personalities. The classic tuxedo is just one option in a sea of possibilities. From tailored suits in an array of colors to more casual ensembles that radiate a laid-back charm, grooms are navigating the fashion landscape with creativity and flair. This chapter is an invitation for grooms to consider the entire spectrum of choices available, ensuring that their attire reflects the authenticity of their personalities and the spirit of the celebration.

Beyond the conventional binary, non-binary and genderqueer individuals are reshaping the landscape of wedding fashion. This is an era where expression knows no bounds. Whether it's a fusion of traditionally masculine and feminine elements or an entirely unique ensemble that defies categorization, the journey is about embracing the freedom to express oneself authentically. It's about navigating fashion choices that transcend traditional gender norms and celebrate the diversity of identities within the LGBTQ+ community.

The concept of "beyond" extends further, encompassing the entire wedding party. As couples celebrate love in all its forms, bridesmaids and groomsmen alike have the opportunity to showcase their unique styles. Coordinating colors and themes offer a cohesive visual narrative, yet this chapter encourages the celebration of individual expressions within the collective celebration.

Navigating fashion choices also involves considering the cultural and familial influences that may shape attire decisions. From traditional ceremonial garments to contemporary interpretations, this is an opportunity to honor heritage while embracing personal style. Cultural attire can serve as a powerful bridge, connecting the past with the present and creating a visual story that resonates with both history and love.

Ultimately, the journey through fashion choices in this chapter is an exploration of possibilities—a celebration of the myriad ways in which individuals and couples express their authentic selves. It's a canvas where personal style meets the celebration of love, and where conventional boundaries give way to a spectrum of choices that reflect the unique beauty of each love story. So, let the exploration unfold, and may your fashion choices be a testament to the individuality, creativity, and authenticity that define your remarkable journey.

Dressing for Comfort and Confidence

In the kaleidoscope of wedding fashion, there's a vital aspect that often takes center stage – the pursuit of dressing for comfort and confidence. This chapter invites you to embark on a journey beyond the aesthetics, recognizing that the garments adorning you on your special day should not only be visually stunning but also imbued with the comfort that allows you to radiate confidence and joy.

Let's begin by acknowledging that comfort is not synonymous with compromise. Today's bridal and groom fashion landscape offers a plethora of options that seamlessly marry style with ease. For brides, this might mean exploring lightweight fabrics that allow for movement, breathable designs that accommodate various climates, and thoughtful tailoring that ensures a perfect fit without sacrificing comfort.

Grooms, too, are presented with an array of choices that prioritize both style and comfort. From suits crafted from breathable materials to tailored ensembles that complement individual body types, the modern groom has the opportunity to select attire that not only looks dashing but feels exceptional throughout the celebration.

The importance of comfort extends beyond the conventional binary, resonating profoundly with non-binary and genderqueer individuals. Dressing for comfort in this context means navigating a world that embraces diverse expressions of gender identity. It involves finding ensembles that align with personal comfort zones, whether it's a fusion of traditionally masculine and feminine elements or an entirely unique creation that defies categorization.

Equally crucial is the comfort felt by bridesmaids, groomsmen, and anyone else standing by your side on the big day. Coordinating attire that considers the diverse preferences and body types within the wedding party ensures that everyone feels at ease, fostering an environment where confidence naturally flourishes.

The quest for comfort is also a consideration for cultural and familial influences shaping attire decisions. Whether it's the weight of traditional ceremonial garments or the cultural significance embedded in certain styles, this chapter invites couples to navigate these choices thoughtfully. Balancing tradition with personal comfort is an art, ensuring that the attire not only pays homage to heritage but also allows individuals to move and celebrate freely.

Furthermore, the journey of dressing for comfort and confidence extends to the concept of gender-affirming attire. For transgender individuals, this may involve selecting garments that align with their affirmed gender identity, fostering a sense of comfort that contributes to an overall positive and affirming experience on the wedding day.

As you navigate this aspect of wedding fashion, consider the practicalities of the day. Long ceremonies, photo sessions, and lively receptions call for attire that not only looks stunning in every frame but also allows you to revel in the moment without discomfort. Think about the venue, the weather, and any activities planned, ensuring that your chosen attire enhances rather than hinders your overall experience.

Ultimately, the journey of dressing for comfort and confidence is a celebration of the individual and collective experiences within the wedding party. It's an acknowledgment that each person's comfort contributes to the collective joy of the celebration. So, as you explore the world of wedding fashion, let comfort be your guiding star, and may your chosen attire not only dazzle the eyes but also envelop you in a cocoon of confidence and ease on your special day.

Customization and Personalization of Attire

As we dive deeper into the realm of wedding attire, an exciting dimension unfolds—customization and personalization. This chapter invites you to explore the vast landscape of possibilities where garments become a canvas for your unique expressions, and wedding fashion transforms into a personalized narrative that echoes the essence of your love story.

Customization is the art of tailoring, quite literally, your attire to your preferences. It's an opportunity to infuse your personality, style, and story into every stitch and seam. For brides, this might involve collaborating with a skilled seamstress to bring a dream gown to life or adding personal touches such as embroidered initials, a significant date, or even a hidden pocket for sentimental items.

Grooms, too, can embark on a journey of sartorial customization. From selecting fabrics that resonate with their personalities to incorporating unique details like custom cufflinks or personalized embroidery on the inside of a jacket, the possibilities are endless. The goal is to create attire that not only looks sharp but also holds layers of significance and meaning.

Non-binary and genderqueer individuals find empowerment in the realm of customization, allowing them to navigate fashion choices that align with their unique gender expressions. The process involves breaking away from traditional norms and working with designers or tailors who understand the importance of creating attire that reflects diverse gender identities.

The wedding party, including bridesmaids and groomsmen, can also partake in the joy of customization. Coordinating attire doesn't mean sacrificing individuality. Consider options like mix-and-match styles, allowing each person to choose elements that suit their preferences while maintaining a cohesive overall look. Personalized accessories, such as custom jewelry or ties, add an extra layer of individual expression.

Cultural and familial influences can be beautifully interwoven into the fabric of customization. Whether it's incorporating traditional patterns, colors, or symbols into the design or repurposing family heirlooms, the process becomes a homage to heritage while ensuring that the attire tells a story that is uniquely yours.

Gender-affirming customization is particularly significant for transgender individuals. This involves tailoring attire to align with affirmed gender identities, ensuring a sense of comfort, affirmation, and joy on the wedding day. Working closely with designers or tailors who understand the nuances of gender expression becomes an integral part of this journey.

Beyond the aesthetics, consider the functional aspects of customization. Are there practical elements that can enhance your wedding day experience? Pockets for convenience, convertible designs for versatility, or detachable elements for a quick transformation are all avenues to explore as you personalize your attire to suit the demands of the day.

Remember that the journey of customization and personalization is a collaborative effort. It involves effective communication with designers, tailors, and anyone involved in bringing your vision to life. Share your inspirations, preferences, and any meaningful elements you'd like to incorporate, ensuring that the final result is a harmonious blend of style, sentiment, and functionality.

In essence, customization and personalization are about making your wedding attire an extension of your identity and love story. It's about transforming garments into tangible expressions of who you are and what your partnership represents. So, let your imagination soar, collaborate with talented creatives, and may your customized attire be a reflection of the beauty, uniqueness, and love that define your remarkable journey.

Bridal Parties and Diverse Attire Choices

In the joyful tapestry of wedding celebrations, the spotlight extends beyond the main couple to illuminate the radiant hues of the bridal party. This section is a celebration of diversity within bridal parties and the delightful journey of embracing a spectrum of attire choices that reflect the individual styles and identities of each participant.

Traditionally, bridesmaids and groomsmen attire has followed a uniform aesthetic. However, the contemporary landscape welcomes a shift towards embracing diversity in both style and gender expression. This evolution is an opportunity for bridesmaids and groomsmen to celebrate their unique identities while contributing to the collective charm of the wedding party.

For bridesmaids, the era of identical dresses is gracefully giving way to a more personalized approach. Mix-and-match styles, varying shades within a color palette, or even distinct patterns offer a delightful visual tapestry that celebrates individuality. This approach ensures that each bridesmaid feels seen and valued, contributing to an atmosphere of inclusivity and joy.

Groomsmen, too, are exploring a broader spectrum of attire choices. From suits in different styles and colors to casual ensembles that align with the overall theme, the possibilities are as diverse as the personalities within the group. This shift allows groomsmen to showcase their individual styles while maintaining a cohesive aesthetic that complements the overall wedding vision.

The concept of gender-inclusive bridal parties is gaining prominence, challenging traditional norms and inviting a more expansive definition of participation. It's no longer bound by gender lines; individuals can stand beside the couple based on their meaningful connections. This shift opens the door for diverse attire choices that reflect the identities of each participant, regardless of gender.

In this journey of diverse attire choices, communication becomes a key element. Open conversations with the bridal party can reveal preferences, comfort levels, and individual styles. This collaborative approach ensures that everyone feels empowered and excited about their chosen attire, contributing to a positive and inclusive atmosphere within the wedding party.

Consider the cultural and familial influences that may shape attire choices within the bridal party. From traditional ceremonial garments to contemporary interpretations, this is an opportunity to honor heritage while embracing personal style. Cultural attire can serve as a beautiful bridge, connecting the diverse backgrounds of the bridal party and contributing to a rich visual narrative.

Beyond the aesthetics, the journey of diverse attire choices within the bridal party is about fostering a sense of community and shared celebration. It's an acknowledgment that each participant brings a unique flavor to the collective experience. Photographs of a diverse and joyous bridal party not only capture the beauty of individual expressions but also become cherished mementos that reflect the inclusivity of the celebration.

As couples navigate this aspect of wedding planning, the focus is on creating an environment where everyone feels celebrated and comfortable. The joy of diverse attire choices is not just in the aesthetics but in the collective spirit of embracing individuality within a shared celebration of love. So, let this chapter unfold with laughter, creativity, and a beautiful kaleidoscope of diverse attire choices that elevate the joy of your wedding day.

Accessible and Gender-Affirming Dress Options

In the ever-evolving landscape of wedding fashion, the call for accessible and gender-affirming dress options resonates profoundly. This section is an exploration of the steps couples can take to ensure that wedding attire is not only visually stunning but also considerate of accessibility needs and inclusive of diverse gender expressions.

Accessibility is a vital consideration in the quest for wedding attire that caters to the diverse needs of all individuals. For individuals with mobility challenges, the journey begins with selecting attire that accommodates their unique needs. Considerations may include the design of the dress or suit, the ease of putting it on and taking it off, and the incorporation of adaptive features such as magnetic closures or adjustable straps. This approach ensures that everyone can participate fully in the joy of the celebration without any hindrance.

Inclusivity extends to gender-affirming dress options that resonate with the diverse expressions of gender identity within the LGBTQ+ community. For transgender individuals, the journey of finding a gender-affirming wedding ensemble is deeply personal. This involves selecting attire that aligns with their affirmed gender identity, taking into account factors such as fit, style, and overall comfort. Working closely with designers or tailors who understand the nuances of gender expression becomes an integral part of this journey.

The bridal party, too, can contribute to the inclusivity of wedding fashion by exploring accessible and gender-affirming dress options. For bridesmaids and groomsmen with diverse needs, considerate choices might involve selecting attire with comfortable silhouettes, accommodating fabrics, and inclusive sizing. This approach ensures that every member of the bridal party can feel confident and at ease throughout the celebration.

Communication plays a crucial role in this journey. Couples are encouraged to have open conversations with their wedding party, ensuring that everyone's needs and preferences are considered. This collaborative approach fosters an atmosphere of inclusivity and allows individuals to express their unique requirements, contributing to a positive and supportive environment.

Cultural and familial influences may intersect with the quest for accessible and gender-affirming dress options. Traditional attire can be adapted to align with accessibility needs and gender expressions, ensuring that cultural significance is preserved while embracing inclusivity. This intersection highlights the richness that arises when diverse influences converge in the celebration of love.

Beyond the attire itself, consider the overall wedding environment. Accessibility features such as ramps, designated seating areas, and gender-neutral restrooms contribute to a more inclusive celebration. These considerations extend hospitality to all guests, ensuring that everyone feels welcome and valued throughout the festivities.

Photography is a powerful medium through which the beauty of accessible and gender-affirming dress options can be celebrated. Thoughtful and inclusive photography captures the essence of each individual's expression, creating lasting memories that reflect the diversity and joy of the celebration.

Ultimately, the journey of accessible and gender-affirming dress options is about creating an inclusive space where everyone can fully participate in the celebration of love. It's a testament to the understanding that every individual, regardless of ability or gender identity, deserves to feel seen, celebrated, and comfortable on such a significant day. So, let this chapter be a guide for couples seeking to weave accessibility and inclusivity into the very fabric of their wedding fashion, creating a celebration that embraces the diversity of love in all its forms.

Chapter 3: Navigating Family Dynamics

Welcome to Chapter 3: Navigating Family Dynamics, a heartfelt exploration into the intricate dance of relationships that is an integral part of the wedding planning journey. As you embark on this chapter, envision it as a gentle guide through the tapestry of family connections, offering insights and strategies to navigate the diverse dynamics that often come to the forefront during the joyous occasion of wedding planning.

Families, with their unique stories, histories, and quirks, bring a wealth of love and complexity to the wedding planning process. This chapter is designed as a companion for couples, a source of support and understanding as they navigate the sometimes challenging, sometimes heartwarming terrain of family dynamics.

Every family has its own dynamic rhythm, shaped by traditions, cultural influences, and individual personalities. Whether you're navigating blended families, bridging cultural gaps, or simply managing the diverse expectations of relatives, this chapter aims to be a reassuring presence, helping you find harmony amid the beautiful chaos.

We delve into the art of communication, offering strategies to foster open and honest dialogues with family members. Effective communication is a cornerstone in navigating family dynamics, allowing couples to express their vision, understand the perspectives of their loved ones, and find common ground that honors both tradition and individuality.

As we explore the complexities that can arise, we also celebrate the moments of connection, the shared laughter, and the collective joy that make family such a vital part of the wedding journey. Whether you're seeking advice on managing differing opinions, addressing sensitive topics, or simply finding ways to include and celebrate every family member, this chapter is a compassionate companion.

Family dynamics extend beyond just the couple's relationship with their immediate families. We consider the broader network of relationships that contribute to the love and support surrounding the couple. From chosen families to close friends who feel like siblings, this chapter is an ode to the expansive definition of family that enriches the wedding planning experience.

In the spirit of creating a celebration that reflects your unique love story, this chapter encourages couples to navigate family dynamics with resilience, empathy, and an understanding heart. It's an invitation to weave the threads of family connections into the beautiful tapestry of your wedding celebration, creating an experience that honors the past, celebrates the present, and looks forward to the shared future. So, let the journey through Chapter 3 unfold, and may it be a guide filled with warmth and wisdom as you navigate the intricate dance of family dynamics on the path to your special day.

Communicating with Family: Tips for Trans Couples

In the delightful and sometimes intricate dance of wedding planning, effective communication with family holds the power to transform potential challenges into moments of understanding, empathy, and shared joy. For trans couples navigating this journey, open and compassionate communication becomes even more crucial, weaving a thread of connection that honors both the couple's vision and the diverse perspectives within their families.

Firstly, embrace the authenticity of your journey. As a trans couple, your wedding is a celebration of love that transcends societal norms. Begin conversations with family from a place of self-assurance, expressing the beauty and uniqueness of your relationship. Share your excitement about the upcoming celebration, framing it as a moment of love, connection, and authenticity.

Educate and share resources. Recognize that some family members may not be familiar with the experiences and language surrounding the transgender community. Provide resources, articles, or personal narratives that offer insight into the journey of transgender individuals. This can create a foundation for understanding and empathy, fostering an environment where questions can be asked and knowledge can grow.

Encourage open dialogue. Communication is a two-way street, and creating a space for family members to express their thoughts and feelings is essential. Let them know that you value their perspectives and are open to hearing their concerns or questions. This openness can pave the way for meaningful conversations that lead to greater understanding and connection.

Set boundaries with compassion. While it's crucial to maintain open communication, it's equally important to set boundaries when needed. If certain topics or comments become uncomfortable or disrespectful, communicate your boundaries with kindness and clarity. Help family members understand the impact of their words or actions, fostering an environment of mutual respect.

Involve them in the planning process. Share the joy of wedding planning by involving family members in aspects of the celebration. Whether it's choosing a venue, selecting décor, or deciding on elements of the ceremony, including family members in the decision-making process can create a sense of shared excitement and investment in the celebration.

Highlight the universal aspects of your wedding. Emphasize the shared values, traditions, and moments of joy that are universal to weddings. While your journey as a trans couple is unique, framing the celebration in the context of love, commitment, and shared joy can create common ground that resonates with family members.

Celebrate milestones and achievements. Share moments of personal growth, achievements, or positive experiences related to your journey. Whether it's milestones in your relationship or personal achievements, these stories can offer a broader perspective on your experiences and highlight the resilience and joy inherent in your journey.

Seek support from allies within the family. Identify family members who are supportive allies and can help bridge understanding with others. Allies can play a crucial role in fostering positive conversations, providing support, and helping to create an environment of acceptance and celebration.

Remember that the journey of communication is ongoing. Building understanding and fostering connection takes time. Be patient with the process, celebrate small victories, and cherish the moments of growth and connection that unfold along the way.

In essence, communicating with family as a trans couple involves embracing authenticity, fostering understanding, and creating a space for shared celebration. It's about weaving a tapestry of connection that reflects the beauty and uniqueness of your love story. So, as you navigate these conversations, may they be filled with warmth, empathy, and a shared vision of love that transcends boundaries.

Handling Potential Challenges with Grace

In the enchanting journey of wedding planning, the path may occasionally present challenges— moments that call for resilience, patience, and a touch of grace. For trans couples navigating family dynamics, these challenges may take various forms, from differing perspectives on gender identity to potential misunderstandings. This section is a gentle exploration into handling these potential challenges with grace, allowing the love and joy of your celebration to shine through.

One key aspect is cultivating resilience. Recognize that not everyone may immediately understand or embrace the journey of a trans couple. There might be questions, hesitations, or even moments of discomfort. Embracing resilience means acknowledging these challenges without allowing them to overshadow the celebration. It involves drawing strength from the love you share and remembering the significance of your union.

Approach challenges with an open heart and a spirit of education. Misunderstandings often stem from lack of awareness or exposure to diverse experiences. If family members express concerns or hold misconceptions, consider it an opportunity for dialogue. Share your experiences, educate them about the transgender community, and help bridge the gap between unfamiliarity and understanding.

Maintain a sense of empathy. Recognize that family members may be navigating their own emotions and perspectives. Approach conversations with a genuine desire to understand their concerns and fears. This empathy can create a space where everyone feels heard and valued, fostering an atmosphere of mutual respect.

Seek support from allies. Allies within the family or close circle can play a vital role in navigating challenges. Identify those who are supportive and understanding, and enlist their help in fostering positive conversations. Allies can provide a bridge between differing perspectives, offering insights and support that contribute to a more harmonious journey.

Consider the power of storytelling. Share your love story and the journey of your relationship with family members. Personal narratives have a unique ability to humanize experiences, making them relatable and fostering empathy. By sharing your story, you invite family members to connect with the genuine emotions and milestones that define your journey.

Practice self-care. Navigating potential challenges can be emotionally taxing. Prioritize self-care to ensure that you and your partner are emotionally resilient. Whether it's taking quiet moments together, seeking support from friends, or engaging in activities that bring joy, self-care is an essential element in maintaining balance and emotional well-being.

Remember that change takes time. Transformations in perspectives and understanding are gradual processes. Be patient with family members and allow them the time and space to evolve in their understanding. Celebrate small victories and moments of growth, recognizing that the journey of acceptance is an ongoing one.

Celebrate your love authentically. Amidst potential challenges, hold onto the authenticity of your love story. Your wedding is a celebration of your unique bond, and every aspect, from the ceremony to the attire, should reflect the authenticity of your relationship. Let the joy and love you share be the guiding light through any challenges that may arise.

Handling potential challenges with grace is a testament to the strength of your love and the resilience of your relationship. It involves embracing each other's differences, fostering understanding, and creating an atmosphere where love can flourish. So, as you navigate these moments, may you do so with grace, patience, and a steadfast commitment to the celebration of your remarkable love.

Building Support Networks: Allies and Advocates

In the intricate tapestry of wedding planning, the importance of building robust support networks cannot be overstated. For trans couples navigating family dynamics, allies and advocates within these networks play a vital role in fostering understanding, providing support, and contributing to an environment where love can truly thrive.

Allies are individuals within your family or close circle who actively support and understand the unique journey of a trans couple. They are the voices of encouragement, the bridges of understanding, and the champions of love. Identifying allies within your family can create a foundation of support that is invaluable in navigating potential challenges.

These allies can play a crucial role in facilitating positive conversations. They can act as mediators, helping to bridge gaps in understanding between the couple and family members who may be navigating unfamiliar terrain. Allies possess the unique ability to articulate perspectives in ways that resonate with those who may be less familiar with the experiences of the transgender community.

The role of allies extends beyond just familial connections. In the broader context of wedding planning, consider seeking allies within the wedding industry—vendors, planners, or consultants who are not only inclusive but also sensitive to the diverse needs of trans couples. Having a team of professionals who understand and respect your journey can contribute to a smoother and more joyous planning process.

Advocates, on the other hand, are individuals who actively work towards creating an inclusive and understanding environment. They go beyond offering personal support and engage in broader conversations to promote awareness and acceptance within the community. Advocates can be instrumental in creating positive change not only within your family but also in the larger social context.

Engaging with advocates may involve participating in community events, attending workshops or support groups, or connecting with organizations that work towards LGBTQ+ inclusivity. These interactions can provide a sense of belonging and empowerment, reinforcing the idea that your love story is part of a broader narrative of diversity and acceptance.

Building support networks is not just about finding individuals who understand your journey; it's also about creating spaces where your love is celebrated. Consider joining online communities or support groups where you can connect with other trans couples, share experiences, and draw strength from a collective sense of understanding. These networks offer a sense of community that can be immensely reassuring during the wedding planning process.

As you build your support network, remember that allies and advocates are allies for a reason—they believe in the beauty and validity of your love. Cultivate these connections with openness and gratitude, recognizing the positive impact they can have not only on your wedding planning journey but also on the broader narrative of acceptance and understanding.

The journey of wedding planning is not meant to be walked alone. It's a collective celebration where allies and advocates become the pillars of support, ensuring that your love story is embraced with warmth, understanding, and celebration. So, as you build these networks, may you find strength, encouragement, and an abundance of love that propels you forward on the path to your remarkable celebration.

Involving Family in Wedding Planning

In the tapestry of wedding planning, involving family members can transform the process into a collaborative and joyous journey. For trans couples navigating family dynamics, inviting your loved ones to be part of the planning not only strengthens familial bonds but also provides opportunities for shared celebrations, understanding, and the creation of lasting memories.

Commence the journey by expressing your desire to involve family members in the wedding planning process. Let them know that their input and presence are valued, creating an atmosphere of inclusivity and shared celebration. This initial communication sets the tone for a collaborative and supportive planning experience.

Consider including family members in key decision-making processes. Whether it's selecting a venue, choosing the theme, or deciding on aspects of the ceremony, involving them in these significant choices fosters a sense of shared investment in the celebration. This collaborative approach ensures that the wedding reflects not only the couple's vision but also incorporates the desires and perspectives of family members.

Encourage family members to share their ideas and traditions. The wedding is an opportunity to merge different elements that hold significance for both the couple and their families. Invite family members to contribute ideas, share traditions, or suggest elements that hold sentimental value. This inclusive approach enriches the celebration with diverse influences, creating a tapestry that reflects the unique story of the couple and their families.

Acknowledge and celebrate familial traditions. Families often carry cherished traditions that have been passed down through generations. Embrace these traditions as part of the wedding celebration, weaving them into the fabric of the ceremony, reception, or other aspects of the event. This gesture not only honors family history but also creates meaningful connections between the past and the present.

Plan family-oriented pre-wedding events. Hosting events such as engagement parties, bridal showers, or rehearsal dinners provides additional opportunities for family members to be actively involved in the celebration. These gatherings create a relaxed and joyful atmosphere where relationships can be strengthened, and everyone can share in the excitement leading up to the wedding day.

Collaborate on DIY projects or personalized elements. Engaging in do-it-yourself (DIY) projects or crafting personalized elements for the wedding can be a delightful way to involve family members. From creating handmade decorations to crafting personalized favors, these collaborative efforts not only add a personal touch to the celebration but also provide enjoyable bonding moments for everyone involved.

Share the joy of the wedding journey through updates and milestones. Keep family members informed about the planning process by sharing updates, milestones, and behind-the-scenes moments. This can be done through regular communications, such as emails, phone calls, or even a shared online platform. Sharing these moments invites family members into the excitement of the journey and allows them to feel connected to the celebration.

Be open to compromise and find common ground. In the midst of planning, it's natural for differing opinions to arise. Approach these moments with an open heart, seeking compromise and finding common ground that aligns with both the couple's vision and the wishes of family members. This collaborative spirit ensures that everyone feels valued and heard throughout the planning process.

Create opportunities for shared experiences. Beyond the logistics of planning, prioritize moments for shared experiences with family members. Whether it's attending bridal expos together, sampling wedding cakes, or participating in cultural or familial traditions, these shared experiences build bonds and contribute to a sense of togetherness leading up to the wedding day.

Involving family in wedding planning is more than a logistical process; it's an opportunity to strengthen connections, create shared memories, and celebrate the journey leading to the union of two lives. As you embark on this collaborative adventure, may it be filled with laughter, love, and the joy of creating a celebration that resonates with the authenticity and warmth of your unique family dynamics.

Navigating Gender Pronouns and Name Changes with Family

Navigating gender pronouns and name changes with family members is a delicate yet pivotal aspect of the wedding planning journey for trans couples. It's a journey of self-discovery, expression, and mutual understanding. As you embark on this path, consider it an opportunity to foster deeper connections with your loved ones by engaging in open and empathetic conversations.

First and foremost, recognize that for some family members, adjusting to new gender pronouns or a name change may require time and education. Understanding and acknowledging this reality is crucial in approaching these conversations with patience and compassion.

Initiate a dialogue with family members about your preferred gender pronouns and name. Frame this conversation in a way that emphasizes the importance of authenticity and self-expression. Share your feelings about the significance of these choices in aligning with your true self and the love you're celebrating in your wedding.

Be prepared to provide information and resources to help family members understand the nuances of gender identity and the importance of using correct pronouns and names. This might involve sharing articles, books, or personal narratives that offer insights into the experiences of transgender individuals. Encourage family members to approach these resources with an open heart, fostering a space for understanding to blossom.

While some family members may readily embrace the change, others may find it challenging due to ingrained habits or preconceived notions. Encourage open dialogue where questions can be asked and answered without judgment. Your willingness to share your journey, experiences, and emotions can provide valuable context that helps family members navigate these changes with sensitivity.

Consider enlisting the support of allies within the family who understand the importance of gender pronouns and name changes. Allies can play a vital role in fostering understanding and can act as advocates during family conversations. Their support can provide an additional layer of reassurance and help facilitate smoother transitions.

Celebrate milestones in your journey together. As you embark on the wedding planning process, share moments of personal growth, self-discovery, and achievements related to your gender identity. These celebrations can be an opportunity to create positive associations with the changes you're undergoing, fostering an atmosphere of joy and understanding within your family.

Acknowledge that mistakes may happen. Family members may inadvertently use incorrect pronouns or names, especially during the adjustment period. Approach these instances with patience and understanding, using them as opportunities for continued dialogue rather than moments of conflict. Reinforce the idea that everyone is learning and growing together.

Consider the emotional impact on family members. Understand that the changes you're undergoing may evoke a range of emotions in your family, including confusion, concern, or even joy. Providing space for family members to express their feelings and concerns fosters an environment of mutual support and understanding.

In the broader context of wedding planning, incorporate your preferred pronouns and name into various elements of the celebration. This might include invitations, ceremony scripts, and other written materials. By integrating these elements, you not only affirm your identity but also create a consistent and supportive environment for your family and guests.

Navigating gender pronouns and name changes with family is a shared journey of understanding, empathy, and mutual respect. It's an opportunity to create connections that transcend language and labels, emphasizing the essence of love and acceptance that lies at the heart of your wedding celebration. As you navigate these conversations, may they be filled with warmth, open-heartedness, and a shared commitment to celebrating the authenticity of each family member on this remarkable journey.

Chapter 4: Trans-Friendly Vendors: Building Your Dream Team

Welcome to Chapter 4: Trans-Friendly Vendors—Building Your Dream Team, where we embark on the exciting quest of assembling a wedding team that not only understands but embraces the unique needs and aspirations of trans couples. In the enchanting landscape of wedding planning, selecting vendors who resonate with your vision is a crucial step toward crafting a celebration that authentically reflects your love story.

This chapter is your companion in navigating the process of curating a dream team that goes beyond professional excellence to create an atmosphere of inclusivity and acceptance. From photographers who capture the essence of your journey to caterers who understand the significance of diverse dietary needs, we explore the spectrum of wedding vendors who are not just allies but advocates for the celebration of love in all its beautiful forms.

In the journey of planning a trans-inclusive wedding, the significance of choosing trans-friendly vendors cannot be overstated. These are the talented individuals and teams who appreciate the uniqueness of your celebration, ensuring that every element aligns with your vision and respects the diverse identities and experiences within the LGBTQ+ community.

We delve into the considerations that go beyond skill and expertise, exploring the importance of open communication, sensitivity, and a genuine commitment to creating a celebration that feels like home. Whether you're envisioning a grand ceremony or an intimate gathering, the vendors you choose play a pivotal role in shaping the ambiance, capturing the moments, and curating an experience that resonates with authenticity.

As you venture into the world of wedding vendors, let this chapter be your guide—a friendly compass that helps you navigate the vast sea of options, ensuring that each professional you choose is not just a vendor but a collaborator in the creation of your dream celebration. So, let's set sail into the realm of trans-friendly vendors, where your dream team awaits, ready to turn your wedding vision into a reality filled with love, understanding, and the magic that makes your love story uniquely yours.

Researching and Identifying Trans-Inclusive Vendors

Embarking on the journey of planning a trans-inclusive wedding is an exciting adventure that involves curating a team of vendors who not only possess skill and expertise but also share a commitment to creating a celebration that embraces diversity and authenticity. The first step in building your dream team is the thoughtful and thorough process of researching and identifying trans-inclusive vendors.

Start your quest by exploring online platforms and wedding directories that emphasize inclusivity. Websites and directories that cater to the LGBTQ+ community often feature vendors who have experience working with diverse couples. These platforms can be a valuable starting point, providing a curated list of professionals who are not just open to, but enthusiastic about, celebrating love in all its forms.

Dive into social media communities and forums where couples share their wedding experiences. Engaging with these communities allows you to tap into the collective wisdom of those who have walked a similar path. Pay attention to the experiences and recommendations shared by trans couples who have celebrated their love, as these insights can guide you toward vendors who have proven themselves to be supportive allies.

Consult with LGBTQ+ organizations and community centers. These organizations often have a network of trans-friendly vendors or can offer recommendations based on their experiences. Reach out to them for guidance and assistance, leveraging the wealth of resources and connections within the community to build a team that aligns with your vision.

Consider the importance of language in vendor communication. Vendors who are truly trans-inclusive are mindful of the language they use in their communications, marketing materials, and contracts. Look for professionals who demonstrate an understanding of diverse gender identities, use inclusive language, and are open to adapting their communication to respect your preferences.

Explore vendor portfolios and testimonials. A vendor's body of work and the experiences of past clients can provide valuable insights into their approach and mindset. Look for evidence of diversity in their portfolios, showcasing weddings that go beyond traditional norms. Testimonials from couples who share similar values can offer assurance that the vendor is genuinely committed to creating an inclusive and affirming celebration.

Reach out and initiate conversations. Once you've identified potential vendors, don't hesitate to reach out and initiate conversations. Pay attention to how they respond to your inquiries, particularly with regards to your specific needs and preferences. A trans-inclusive vendor will approach these conversations with openness, empathy, and a genuine interest in understanding and celebrating your unique love story.

Ask direct questions about their experience and approach. During your conversations with potential vendors, ask direct questions about their experience working with trans couples. Inquire about their understanding of diverse gender identities, their flexibility in accommodating specific requests, and their commitment to creating a celebration that feels inclusive and affirming.

Trust your instincts. As you navigate the process of researching and identifying trans-inclusive vendors, trust your instincts. Pay attention to how you feel during your interactions with each professional. A vendor who is genuinely committed to inclusivity will not only have the skills you seek but will also create an atmosphere of trust, understanding, and excitement about bringing your vision to life.

Remember, building your dream team is not just about finding skilled professionals; it's about finding allies who share your commitment to celebrating love authentically. So, let the journey of researching and identifying trans-inclusive vendors be a joyful exploration, bringing you one step closer to crafting a celebration that reflects the unique beauty of your love story.

Interviewing and Selecting Supportive Wedding Professionals

Interviewing and selecting supportive wedding professionals is a pivotal step in bringing your dream celebration to life. Beyond the technical aspects of their craft, it's crucial to ensure that the vendors you choose are not only trans-inclusive but also genuinely committed to understanding and celebrating your unique love story. Here's a guide on how to navigate the interview and selection process with warmth, curiosity, and a discerning eye.

Initiate conversations that go beyond logistics. When you connect with potential vendors, take the opportunity to delve into meaningful conversations that go beyond the typical questions about services and prices. Share your vision for the wedding, your journey as a couple, and the values that are important to you. A trans-inclusive vendor will engage with these aspects of your story, demonstrating a genuine interest in understanding the nuances that make your celebration uniquely yours.

Ask about their experience and approach with trans couples. During the interview, inquire about the vendor's experience working with trans couples. Ask about specific instances where they've accommodated unique requests or navigated challenges to ensure an inclusive celebration. A supportive professional will openly share their experiences and demonstrate an eagerness to create a wedding environment that is respectful, understanding, and affirming.

Pay attention to language and communication style. Language is a powerful indicator of a vendor's commitment to inclusivity. Take note of how they communicate, both verbally and in written form. A trans-inclusive vendor will use language that is respectful of diverse gender identities and expressions. They will be open to adapting their communication to align with your preferred pronouns and names, creating an atmosphere of acceptance.

Discuss your specific needs and preferences. Share the specific needs and preferences that are important to you as a trans couple. Whether it's related to attire, ceremony language, or any other aspect of the celebration, a supportive vendor will listen attentively, ask clarifying questions, and express a willingness to tailor their services to align with your vision. This collaborative approach ensures that your unique needs are not just acknowledged but celebrated.

Explore their portfolio and references. Take a close look at the vendor's portfolio, paying attention to the diversity of weddings they have been a part of. Look for evidence that they have successfully worked with couples who have celebrated love in various ways. Additionally, request references from past clients, especially those who may share similar values or experiences. Hearing about the vendor's impact from those who have walked a similar path can provide valuable insights.

Consider their adaptability and flexibility. The ability of a vendor to adapt and be flexible is essential in ensuring that your unique needs are met. Inquire about their approach to handling unexpected situations or changes to the plan. A vendor who is adaptable and flexible will approach these moments with creativity and a solution-oriented mindset, contributing to a smoother and more enjoyable planning process.

Trust your instincts and assess their enthusiasm. Throughout the interview process, trust your instincts. Pay attention to how you feel during your interactions with each vendor. An enthusiastic and genuinely supportive professional will convey a sense of excitement about being a part of your celebration. They will express a genuine commitment to ensuring that your wedding is a true reflection of your love story.

Remember, the vendors you choose are not just professionals—they are collaborators in the creation of a celebration that resonates with authenticity and inclusivity. The interview and selection process is an opportunity to build a team of individuals who not only understand the technicalities of their craft but also share in the joy of celebrating love in all its beautiful forms. So, let the conversations be guided by warmth, curiosity, and a shared commitment to crafting a wedding experience that feels uniquely and beautifully yours.

Working with Wedding Planners and Coordinators

Navigating the intricate tapestry of wedding planning can be both exciting and overwhelming, and enlisting the support of a wedding planner or coordinator can be a game-changer. When working with wedding professionals in these roles, it's essential to find individuals who not only possess the expertise to bring your vision to life but also understand and celebrate the unique needs of trans couples.

In your search for a wedding planner or coordinator, seek professionals who exude warmth, empathy, and a genuine commitment to inclusivity. These qualities go beyond the logistical aspects of planning and contribute to a collaborative and affirming wedding experience.

Communication is key in any successful planning process, and this holds especially true when working with a wedding planner or coordinator. Look for professionals who actively listen to your desires, concerns, and unique considerations as a trans couple. A skilled planner will create an open and inviting space for dialogue, ensuring that your vision is not just understood but celebrated throughout the planning journey.

When interviewing potential wedding planners, inquire about their experience working with trans couples. A seasoned professional will share examples of past weddings where they've navigated diverse needs and preferences. Their experiences should demonstrate a commitment to creating inclusive celebrations that authentically represent each couple's love story.

A trans-aware wedding planner will understand the significance of language and terminology in wedding planning. They will be open to using gender-inclusive language, adapting their communication style to respect your preferred pronouns and names, and creating an atmosphere of acceptance. This attention to language contributes to an environment where every detail of your celebration is thoughtfully considered and reflective of your unique identity.

Consider the planner's network of vendors. A well-connected wedding planner often collaborates with a network of vendors, and a trans-aware planner will curate a team that shares their commitment to inclusivity. Inquire about their relationships with vendors and how they ensure that each professional they recommend aligns with the values of celebrating love in all its forms.

Discuss how the planner approaches potential challenges related to gender identity and expression. The journey of wedding planning may involve moments that require sensitivity and understanding, particularly concerning gender identity and expression. A trans-aware wedding planner will have strategies in place for navigating these challenges, ensuring that the planning process remains respectful and affirming.

Explore the planner's approach to incorporating personal and cultural elements. A wedding is a deeply personal celebration, and a trans-aware planner will appreciate the importance of incorporating personal and cultural elements that hold significance for you as a couple. Whether it's related to attire, ceremony rituals, or other aspects, a skilled planner will work to weave these elements seamlessly into the fabric of your celebration.

Look for a planner who values and prioritizes your privacy. The journey of a trans couple may involve sharing personal and intimate details, and a trans-aware wedding planner will prioritize your privacy and confidentiality. Discuss how the planner approaches handling sensitive information and ensures a secure and respectful planning process.

Consider their adaptability and flexibility. Wedding plans can evolve, and unforeseen circumstances may arise. A skilled planner will approach changes or adjustments with adaptability and flexibility, working collaboratively with you to find solutions that align with your vision and unique circumstances.

Trust your instincts and assess their enthusiasm. Throughout the interview process, trust your instincts. Pay attention to how you feel during your interactions with the wedding planner. An enthusiastic and genuinely supportive professional will convey a sense of excitement about being a part of your celebration. They will express a commitment to ensuring that your wedding planning experience is not just efficient but also joyous and affirming.

Working with a wedding planner or coordinator who understands and celebrates the unique needs of trans couples can transform the planning journey into a collaborative and joyful experience. May you find a skilled professional who not only possesses the expertise to bring your vision to life but also shares in the joy of celebrating love authentically and inclusively.

Tips for Trans-Friendly Communication with Vendors

In the intricate dance of wedding planning, effective and respectful communication with vendors is a key ingredient for a smooth and affirming experience, especially for trans couples navigating the process. Establishing trans-friendly communication sets the stage for a collaborative and inclusive journey, ensuring that every detail of your celebration aligns with your vision and identity.

First and foremost, be open about your identity and preferences. From the initial contact with vendors, openly share your gender identity, preferred pronouns, and any specific preferences related to your celebration. This transparent communication lays the foundation for a respectful and inclusive planning process, fostering an environment where vendors can appreciate the unique elements that make your love story authentically yours.

Clearly communicate your vision for the celebration. Paint a vivid picture of your wedding vision, including the atmosphere, themes, and elements that hold personal significance. The more vendors understand your vision, the better equipped they are to align their services and contributions with your unique preferences. Share the details that matter most to you, whether it's related to attire, ceremony language, or other aspects of the celebration.

Educate vendors on trans-inclusive language and terminology. Take the opportunity to educate vendors about trans-inclusive language and terminology. Be proactive in sharing your preferred pronouns and names, and encourage vendors to adapt their communication accordingly. This educational approach contributes to a wedding experience where language is thoughtful, respectful, and affirming of diverse gender identities.

Ask vendors about their experience with trans couples. During your interactions with vendors, inquire about their experience working with trans couples. Ask for examples of weddings they've been a part of that celebrated diverse gender identities and expressions. A vendor who is experienced and trans-aware will share stories that highlight their commitment to inclusivity and their ability to navigate the unique considerations of trans couples.

Clarify any specific needs related to attire. If you have specific preferences or considerations related to attire, communicate these clearly with vendors. Whether it involves non-traditional attire, gender-neutral options, or customization to align with your unique style, vendors appreciate clear guidance to ensure that the attire choices contribute to the authenticity of your celebration.

Establish an open line of communication for questions and concerns. Create a welcoming space for vendors to ask questions and express any concerns they may have. An open line of communication fosters a collaborative environment where vendors can seek clarity on your preferences and address any potential challenges with sensitivity and understanding.

Be proactive in addressing potential challenges. Anticipate potential challenges related to gender identity and expression, and address them proactively with vendors. This may involve discussing how to handle situations where someone may use incorrect pronouns or names, ensuring that vendors are prepared to navigate these moments with grace and understanding.

Encourage vendors to share their ideas and expertise. While your vision is central to the planning process, vendors bring a wealth of expertise and creativity to the table. Encourage them to share their ideas and suggestions, particularly in areas where their experience can enhance the celebration. This collaborative approach ensures that the planning process benefits from the diverse perspectives of both the couple and the vendors.

Prioritize ongoing communication and updates. Maintain regular communication with vendors throughout the planning process, providing updates on any changes, milestones, or evolving preferences. This ensures that vendors are kept in the loop and can adjust their services accordingly. Ongoing communication contributes to a collaborative and flexible planning experience that adapts to the evolving needs of the celebration.

Trust your instincts and assess their responsiveness. As you communicate with vendors, trust your instincts. Pay attention to how you feel during your interactions, and assess the responsiveness of each vendor. A responsive and trans-aware vendor will not only acknowledge your preferences but will actively engage with your vision, contributing to a planning process that feels collaborative, supportive, and celebratory.

Effective and trans-friendly communication with vendors is a cornerstone of a wedding planning process that celebrates love in all its beautiful forms. By fostering open dialogue, educating vendors on trans-inclusive considerations, and maintaining ongoing communication, you create a collaborative and affirming environment where every detail of your celebration reflects the warmth and authenticity of your unique love story. May your wedding planning journey be filled with communication that is thoughtful, joyful, and reflective of the beautiful diversity that defines your love.

Chapter 5: Ceremony and Rituals with Meaning

Welcome to Chapter 5: Ceremony and Rituals with Meaning, a heartwarming exploration into the soulful tapestry of wedding ceremonies that go beyond tradition to embrace the unique stories and identities of trans couples. In this chapter, we embark on a journey of discovery, reimagining the rituals that bind two hearts in love, celebrating the beauty of diversity, and infusing every moment with profound meaning.

Your wedding ceremony is a canvas on which the brushstrokes of your love story are painted. It's a sacred space where every word spoken, every ritual performed, and every gesture exchanged holds the power to reflect the essence of your unique journey as a couple. This chapter is your guide to crafting a ceremony that feels not only deeply personal but authentically and inclusively yours.

We delve into the art of infusing meaning into every aspect of your ceremony. From the words spoken by officiants to the rituals that symbolize unity, we explore how to create a ceremony that resonates with the authentic identity and love shared by trans couples. This is a celebration that goes beyond conformity, inviting you to reimagine and redefine wedding traditions in a way that feels profoundly meaningful.

Throughout this chapter, you'll discover inspiration for crafting a ceremony that aligns with your vision, values, and the rich tapestry of your love story. Whether you're envisioning a ceremony that honors cultural traditions, embraces gender-neutral language, or introduces unique rituals that reflect your identity, this chapter is a celebration of the diverse ways in which love can be expressed and celebrated.

So, let the journey into Ceremony and Rituals with Meaning be a joyful exploration, a canvas on which you paint the story of your love in vibrant hues. May the words spoken, the rituals performed, and the moments shared during your ceremony be a reflection of the deep, authentic, and beautifully diverse love that defines your union. Welcome to a chapter where your ceremony is not just a moment; it's a masterpiece, a living testament to the extraordinary love you share.

Developing Trans-Inclusive Wedding Rituals

Creating a wedding ceremony that feels truly inclusive and reflective of the identities and experiences of trans couples is a beautiful journey into the heart of love and commitment. In this section, we explore the art of developing trans-inclusive wedding rituals—rituals that go beyond tradition to embrace the unique stories and expressions of each couple.

Start by envisioning the essence of your love story. Before delving into specific rituals, take a moment to reflect on the essence of your love. What defines your journey as a couple? What experiences, values, and symbols hold profound meaning for you? By understanding the core of your love story, you lay the foundation for creating rituals that authentically reflect your unique identity as a trans couple.

Consider incorporating gender-neutral language. Language holds immense power in shaping the tone of your ceremony. Embrace gender-neutral language that transcends traditional norms and reflects the diversity of gender identities. From vows to readings, weaving inclusive language into your ceremony creates an atmosphere of acceptance and celebration of the rich tapestry of identities within the LGBTQ+ community.

Explore rituals that symbolize unity and connection. Rituals have the power to symbolize the unity and connection between you and your partner. Consider incorporating rituals that go beyond the conventional, such as unity ceremonies that involve blending different elements, creating art together, or symbolizing the merging of two unique paths into one shared journey. These rituals become poignant expressions of your commitment to walking through life together, celebrating both your individuality and your shared bond.

Celebrate your cultural heritage. If you and your partner come from diverse cultural backgrounds, infuse elements of your heritage into the ceremony. This could involve incorporating traditional attire, rituals, or symbols that hold deep cultural significance. Celebrating your cultural heritage not only adds richness to your ceremony but also honors the diverse tapestry of your identities.

Craft personalized vows that speak your truth. Vows are the heart of your ceremony, and crafting personalized vows allows you to speak your truth and express the unique promises and commitments you're making to each other. Share your journey, your dreams, and the qualities you cherish in one another. Personalized vows are a powerful way to celebrate your love story and create a ceremony that is deeply personal and trans-inclusive.

Involve loved ones in meaningful roles. Consider involving loved ones in meaningful roles during the ceremony. This could include family members or friends participating in readings, blessings, or symbolic gestures. By including those closest to you in the ceremony, you create a sense of community and support that is essential in celebrating the unique love story of a trans couple.

Consult with your officiant on inclusive language and understanding. Your officiant plays a central role in guiding the ceremony. Have open and honest conversations with your officiant about your preferences, including the use of inclusive language and an understanding of the unique aspects of your love story. A trans-inclusive officiant will work collaboratively with you to ensure that the ceremony aligns with your vision and values.

Consider rituals that reflect personal journeys. The journey of a trans individual often involves personal growth, self-discovery, and courage. Consider incorporating rituals that symbolize these journeys, such as the lighting of candles to represent personal transformation or the exchange of symbolic objects that reflect the strength and resilience of your path. These rituals become powerful expressions of the beauty found in personal growth and authenticity.

Embrace rituals that celebrate chosen families. Many trans individuals have chosen families that play significant roles in their lives. Embrace rituals that celebrate and honor these chosen families, whether through special acknowledgments, readings, or symbolic gestures. Recognizing the importance of chosen families contributes to a ceremony that authentically reflects the support networks that shape your lives.

In the development of trans-inclusive wedding rituals, the key is to infuse every element with meaning and authenticity. Your ceremony becomes a canvas on which your unique love story is painted, celebrated, and honored. By embracing inclusive language, exploring diverse rituals, and weaving personal journeys into the fabric of the ceremony, you create a transformative experience that goes beyond tradition to authentically celebrate the beautiful diversity of love. May your wedding rituals be a reflection of the profound and extraordinary love that defines your union.

Incorporating Cultural and Spiritual Elements

In the tapestry of love and commitment, cultural and spiritual elements woven into a wedding ceremony add layers of richness and meaning. In this section, we explore the art of incorporating cultural and spiritual elements into your ceremony, creating a celebration that not only honors tradition but also resonates deeply with the identities of trans couples.

Begin by embracing the diversity of your cultural backgrounds. As a trans couple, you may come from different cultural backgrounds, each with its own traditions and rituals. Embrace this diversity and consider incorporating elements from both backgrounds into your ceremony. Whether it's traditional attire, customs, or symbolic gestures, blending cultural elements creates a ceremony that beautifully reflects the mosaic of your identities.

Consult with cultural advisors or officiants. When incorporating cultural elements, consulting with cultural advisors or officiants who specialize in your respective backgrounds can provide valuable insights. These experts can offer guidance on the significance of specific traditions, ensure respectful execution, and help weave cultural threads seamlessly into the fabric of your ceremony.

Explore rituals that symbolize unity. Many cultural and spiritual traditions include rituals that symbolize unity and connection. From handfasting ceremonies to the exchange of symbolic objects, these rituals can be adapted to reflect the unique journey of a trans couple. Consider rituals that resonate with both your cultural backgrounds, creating a harmonious and meaningful representation of your union.

Infuse cultural attire into your celebration. Traditional attire carries deep cultural significance and can be a powerful way to honor your heritage. Consider incorporating elements of cultural attire into your wedding attire, paying homage to your roots and celebrating the beauty of your identities. This could involve garments, accessories, or symbolic colors that hold cultural meaning.

Celebrate cultural holidays or festivals. If your wedding coincides with a cultural holiday or festival, consider incorporating elements of the celebration into your ceremony. This could involve rituals, decorations, or blessings associated with the occasion. Celebrating cultural holidays adds a layer of joy and festivity to your wedding, creating a memorable and culturally rich experience.

Adapt religious traditions with sensitivity. For couples with religious backgrounds, adapting religious traditions with sensitivity is a thoughtful approach. Engage in open and honest conversations with religious leaders or officiants to explore ways to incorporate elements of your faith into the ceremony while respecting your identities. This collaborative approach ensures a ceremony that aligns with your beliefs and values.

Include cultural readings, blessings, or prayers. Cultural readings, blessings, or prayers can add depth and resonance to your ceremony. Choose texts or verses that hold personal significance, reflecting the values and teachings of your cultural backgrounds. These elements become profound expressions of your commitment, bridging cultural traditions with the celebration of your love.

Incorporate music and dance from your cultures. Music and dance are powerful expressions of culture, and incorporating traditional songs or dances into your ceremony can create a vibrant and celebratory atmosphere. Whether it's a traditional dance during the processional or a cultural song performed during a key moment, these elements infuse your ceremony with the rhythms and melodies of your heritage.

Honor ancestors and familial traditions. Ancestors and familial traditions play a significant role in many cultures. Consider incorporating elements that honor ancestors, such as a moment of reflection, a symbolic gesture, or the inclusion of family heirlooms. Recognizing and paying homage to ancestral roots adds a profound layer of meaning to your ceremony.

Personalize cultural elements to reflect your journey. While embracing cultural traditions, feel empowered to personalize them to reflect your unique journey as a trans couple. Whether it's adapting rituals, choosing specific cultural elements that resonate with you, or infusing personal touches into traditional customs, make the ceremony a true reflection of your love story.

Incorporating cultural and spiritual elements into your wedding ceremony is a celebration of identity, heritage, and love. It's a journey into the heart of tradition, where the beauty of diversity is celebrated and woven into the fabric of your love story. May your ceremony be a harmonious blend of cultural richness, spiritual depth, and the extraordinary love that defines your union.

Writing Personalized Vows: A Guide for Trans Couples

Crafting personalized vows is a deeply intimate and powerful aspect of your wedding ceremony, offering you and your partner the opportunity to express the unique promises and commitments that define your love. In this section, we delve into the art of writing personalized vows, providing a guide specifically tailored for trans couples.

Start by reflecting on your love journey. Before putting pen to paper, take a moment to reflect on the journey that has brought you and your partner to this significant moment. Consider the milestones, challenges, and joys you've shared as a couple. Your reflections will serve as the foundation for crafting vows that authentically capture the essence of your love story.

Embrace your authentic voice. Your vows are an expression of your true self, and as a trans couple, embracing your authentic voice is paramount. Allow yourself the freedom to use language that feels genuine and reflects your identity. Whether it's the use of gender-neutral pronouns or incorporating specific terms that resonate with your experience, let your vows be a reflection of your unique voice and expression.

Express your love in your own words. While inspiration can be drawn from poems, songs, or quotes, the heart of your vows lies in your own words. Speak from the heart, using language that resonates with you and your partner. Express the depth of your love, the qualities you cherish in one another, and the promises you are making as you embark on this journey together.

Acknowledge the uniqueness of your love story. Your vows are an opportunity to celebrate the uniqueness of your love story as a trans couple. Acknowledge the significance of your journey, the strength of your connection, and the beauty found in your identities. By recognizing and celebrating the unique elements of your love, your vows become a testament to the extraordinary nature of your relationship.

Consider incorporating shared experiences. Infuse your vows with shared experiences that hold special meaning for both of you. Whether it's referencing a memorable moment in your relationship, acknowledging the support you've provided for one another, or expressing gratitude for the shared journey of self-discovery, incorporating these experiences adds a personal and intimate touch to your vows.

Discuss your vows with your partner. While the vows themselves are a personal expression, consider discussing certain aspects with your partner to ensure a harmonious and cohesive ceremony. This could involve agreeing on the overall tone of the vows, deciding on any common themes, or discussing the level of detail you both feel comfortable sharing. Open communication ensures that your vows complement each other and contribute to a unified ceremony.

Celebrate growth and resilience. The journey of a trans individual often involves personal growth, self-discovery, and resilience. Acknowledge and celebrate these aspects in your vows. Share how your partner's support has been a source of strength, express gratitude for the growth you've experienced together, and celebrate the resilience that defines your journey as a couple.

Include promises that resonate with your journey. Your vows are an opportunity to make promises that hold profound meaning for you and your partner. Consider including promises that resonate with your journey, whether it involves promises of unwavering support during times of transition, commitments to continued growth and understanding, or pledges to celebrate the beauty found in your identities.

Seek inspiration from shared interests. Draw inspiration from shared interests, hobbies, or passions that define your relationship. Whether it's a mutual love for a particular activity, a shared goal, or a common vision for the future, incorporating these elements into your vows adds a layer of connection and celebration of the shared aspects of your life.

Express gratitude and appreciation. Take a moment in your vows to express gratitude and appreciation for your partner. Acknowledge the ways in which they have enriched your life, supported you on your journey, and brought joy and love into your world. Gratitude becomes a beautiful thread woven into the fabric of your vows, creating a ceremony that is rooted in appreciation and love.

Writing personalized vows is a heartfelt and joyous endeavor, allowing you and your partner to articulate the depth of your love and commitment. As a trans couple, these vows become a unique expression of your identities, your journey, and the extraordinary love that binds you together. May your words resonate with authenticity, may your promises echo with sincerity, and may your vows be a beautiful testament to the extraordinary journey of love you are embarking on.

Creating a Gender-Affirming Ceremony Space

Creating a gender-affirming ceremony space is a thoughtful and impactful way to ensure that your wedding ceremony is inclusive, respectful, and celebratory of diverse gender identities. In this section, we explore the elements and considerations that contribute to crafting a ceremony space that honors the identities of trans individuals and couples.

Begin by choosing an inclusive venue. Selecting a venue that is not only welcoming but also actively inclusive sets the stage for a gender-affirming ceremony. Seek out venues that have a track record of embracing diversity, understanding the importance of using inclusive language, and respecting the unique needs of trans couples. Discuss your preferences with venue staff to ensure a supportive and affirming environment.

Communicate openly with vendors and officiants. Establish open lines of communication with your vendors and officiant, discussing your expectations for a gender-affirming ceremony space. Share your preferred pronouns, any specific requests related to language and terminology, and your vision for an inclusive atmosphere. A supportive vendor team will appreciate your openness and work collaboratively to create an environment that aligns with your values.

Consider the language used in your ceremony. Language is a powerful tool in creating a gender-affirming space. Work with your officiant to choose language that is inclusive and respectful of diverse gender identities. This may involve using gender-neutral terms, adapting traditional language, or incorporating specific terms that resonate with your identities. Your ceremony becomes a space where language reflects the rich tapestry of gender diversity.

Incorporate symbols of inclusivity. Infuse your ceremony space with symbols that celebrate inclusivity. This could involve incorporating LGBTQ+ pride symbols, trans pride colors, or other symbols that hold personal significance for you as a couple. These symbols become visual affirmations of the diverse identities present in the ceremony space and contribute to a welcoming atmosphere.

Provide gender-neutral restrooms. Ensure that the venue provides gender-neutral restrooms to create an inclusive environment for all attendees. Gender-neutral restrooms contribute to a ceremony space that acknowledges and respects diverse gender identities, providing a simple yet impactful way to create an affirming atmosphere.

Consider seating arrangements. When planning seating arrangements for your ceremony, consider creating a layout that accommodates diverse needs. Provide options for seating that allow attendees to choose spaces where they feel most comfortable. This may include flexible seating arrangements, the inclusion of designated areas, or other considerations that respect the diverse identities of your guests.

Offer support resources. Recognize that weddings can be emotional and sometimes challenging events. Consider providing resources such as informational pamphlets, contact information for LGBTQ+ support organizations, or other materials that offer support and guidance for attendees. This thoughtful gesture ensures that everyone present feels supported and valued.

Celebrate diverse love stories. Use your ceremony space as a platform to celebrate diverse love stories. Consider incorporating readings, stories, or elements that reflect the richness of LGBTQ+ love and relationships. Whether through personal anecdotes, historical references, or literary excerpts, celebrating diverse love stories contributes to a ceremony space that honors the beautiful spectrum of identities present.

Encourage attendees to be mindful. In the spirit of creating a gender-affirming space, encourage all attendees to be mindful of language, pronouns, and the diverse identities present. Consider including a brief statement in your ceremony program or having your officiant make an announcement encouraging respect and inclusivity. This proactive approach fosters an atmosphere where everyone feels seen, respected, and celebrated.

Create a safe space for self-expression. Your ceremony is a celebration of love, and creating a safe space for self-expression ensures that everyone can fully participate in the joyous occasion. Consider incorporating elements that allow attendees to express their identities, whether through attire, accessories, or other means. This freedom of self-expression contributes to a ceremony space where everyone feels authentically represented.

By incorporating these considerations into your wedding ceremony, you contribute to the creation of a gender-affirming space that is welcoming, respectful, and celebratory of diverse gender identities. May your ceremony be a reflection of the beautiful spectrum of love and identity, where everyone present feels seen, celebrated, and embraced in the warmth of your love.

Engaging Guests in Meaningful Trans-Inclusive Rituals

Engaging your guests in meaningful trans-inclusive rituals is a beautiful way to foster a sense of community, celebration, and inclusivity during your wedding ceremony. In this section, we explore how to create a shared experience that actively involves your guests in celebrating the unique journey of trans couples.

Begin by setting the tone for inclusivity. From the outset, communicate the values of inclusivity and respect to your guests. Consider including a brief note in your wedding program or having your officiant make an announcement that encourages everyone to embrace diversity, use inclusive language, and be mindful of the varied identities present. This sets a positive tone for the ceremony and invites guests to participate in creating an affirming atmosphere.

Incorporate a communal blessing or affirmation. Create a moment during the ceremony where guests can collectively offer a blessing or affirmation for the couple. This could involve a brief period where guests express their well-wishes, offer positive energy, or share words of support. By involving the entire gathering, you create a powerful and inclusive energy that resonates throughout the ceremony.

Encourage guests to share personal reflections. Invite guests to share personal reflections or anecdotes related to love, commitment, and the celebration of diverse identities. This could take the form of an open mic session, written notes placed in a communal vessel, or a designated space for guests to contribute their thoughts. The act of sharing personal reflections adds a layer of depth and personal connection to the ceremony, emphasizing the communal celebration of love.

Include a unity ceremony with guest participation. Consider incorporating a unity ceremony that actively involves your guests. This could be a symbolic ritual where guests contribute to a collaborative artwork, create a communal blessing or wish tree, or participate in a group gesture that symbolizes unity and support. The involvement of guests in a unity ceremony creates a shared experience that goes beyond traditional spectatorship.

Create a moment of acknowledgment and gratitude. Dedicate a moment in the ceremony to acknowledge and express gratitude for the support of your guests. This could involve a verbal expression of thanks, the inclusion of a written statement in your program, or a symbolic gesture of appreciation. Recognizing the importance of your guests' presence and support contributes to a sense of community and shared celebration.

Offer pronoun stickers or badges. To foster a gender-inclusive atmosphere, consider providing pronoun stickers or badges for guests to wear. This simple yet effective gesture allows guests to communicate their pronouns and encourages respectful language use. It also sends a clear message that the celebration is intentionally trans-inclusive, creating a space where everyone's identity is acknowledged and respected.

Incorporate an interactive element into the ceremony program. Include an interactive element in your ceremony program that engages guests in a meaningful way. This could be a trivia game about LGBTQ+ history and achievements, a collaborative art project, or a thought-provoking question for reflection. By incorporating an interactive component, you encourage guests to actively participate and invest in the ceremony experience.

Share resources for allyship and understanding. Consider providing informational resources on allyship and understanding LGBTQ+ identities in your ceremony space. This could take the form of pamphlets, a display table with educational materials, or a website link included in your program. Sharing resources encourages guests to deepen their understanding of diverse identities and fosters a culture of inclusivity.

Encourage guests to use inclusive language. Throughout the ceremony, encourage guests to use inclusive language that respects diverse gender identities. This could be communicated through the officiant's remarks, included in the program, or mentioned in a brief announcement. By fostering an atmosphere where inclusive language is valued, you create a space where everyone feels seen and respected.

Celebrate the diversity of love. Emphasize the celebration of diverse love stories as a central theme of the ceremony. Whether through readings, symbolic gestures, or visual displays, highlight the beauty found in the varied experiences and identities within the LGBTQ+ community. By celebrating the diversity of love, you create a ceremony space that honors and uplifts the rich tapestry of identities present.

Engaging your guests in meaningful trans-inclusive rituals transforms your wedding ceremony into a shared experience of love, celebration, and community. By actively involving guests in the celebration, you foster an atmosphere of inclusivity, respect, and joy that resonates throughout the gathering. May your wedding be a testament to the power of communal celebration, where everyone present feels a deep connection to the love being celebrated and the diverse identities being honored.

Chapter 6: Legalities and Documentation

Welcome to Chapter 6: Legalities and Documentation. While planning a wedding is undoubtedly an exciting and joyous endeavor, it's equally important to navigate the legal aspects that formalize your union. This chapter is your guide to understanding the legalities and documentation involved in the journey toward marriage, with a focus on ensuring that the process is smooth, inclusive, and tailored to the needs of trans couples.

In the pages that follow, we'll delve into the legal requirements and considerations specific to trans individuals and couples. From obtaining the necessary documentation to understanding name changes and gender marker updates, we'll walk you through each step of the process with clarity and compassion.

Navigating the legal landscape of marriage can sometimes be a complex journey, but fear not – this chapter is here to demystify the process. We'll explore how to ensure that your marriage is legally recognized, providing you with the tools and insights needed to embark on this aspect of your wedding planning journey confidently.

As we venture into the legalities and documentation surrounding trans weddings, our aim is to empower you with knowledge and resources. Whether you're considering a name change, updating identification documents, or simply understanding the legal requirements for your union, this chapter is designed to be your reliable companion.

Remember, the legal aspects of your wedding are an integral part of the celebration of your love. We encourage you to approach this chapter with a sense of curiosity and readiness to navigate the legal landscape with confidence. Your love story is unique, and so too should be the legal recognition of your union. Let's embark on this journey together, ensuring that your wedding is not only a beautiful celebration of love but also a legally sound and inclusive expression of your commitment.

Understanding Marriage Laws for Trans Couples

Understanding marriage laws is a crucial aspect of planning a wedding, and for trans couples, it involves navigating legal considerations that are both unique and significant. In this section, we'll explore the key elements of marriage laws for trans couples, providing insights and guidance to ensure that your union is not only celebrated with love but also recognized and protected under the law.

Marriage laws vary by jurisdiction, and it's essential to familiarize yourself with the specific regulations in the location where you plan to get married. One of the primary considerations for trans couples is the legal recognition of gender identity. Laws regarding gender markers on identification documents, such as driver's licenses or passports, may impact the documentation required for marriage.

In many places, the legal recognition of gender identity has evolved, allowing individuals to update their identification documents to reflect their affirmed gender. However, the process and requirements for updating these documents can differ. It's advisable to check with the relevant government agencies to understand the steps involved, the documentation needed, and any waiting periods that may apply.

When it comes to obtaining a marriage license, trans couples should be aware of the specific requirements set by the jurisdiction. Some areas may have outdated or restrictive language in their marriage laws, using terms that don't fully encompass the diversity of gender identities. It's essential to advocate for inclusivity and, if necessary, seek legal advice to navigate any challenges related to terminology or requirements.

Name changes are another consideration for trans individuals planning to get married. Whether you've already legally changed your name or plan to do so as part of the marriage process, understanding the legal implications and requirements is crucial. Some jurisdictions may have specific procedures for name changes, while others may allow individuals to choose the name they wish to use without additional legal steps.

Seeking legal advice or consulting with organizations that specialize in LGBTQ+ rights can be valuable resources for trans couples navigating marriage laws. Legal professionals with expertise in this area can provide personalized guidance based on the specific laws and regulations in your jurisdiction. Additionally, LGBTQ+ advocacy organizations often offer resources and support to individuals facing legal challenges related to their gender identity or sexual orientation.

In some cases, trans individuals may encounter obstacles when attempting to update their identification documents or face discriminatory practices when seeking a marriage license. Understanding your rights and seeking support from organizations that specialize in LGBTQ+ legal advocacy can be instrumental in addressing and challenging discriminatory practices.

As you embark on the journey of marriage, remember that you have the right to a celebration that is not only joyous but also legally recognized. By staying informed about the marriage laws in your jurisdiction, advocating for inclusivity, and seeking appropriate legal advice when needed, you can ensure that your union is not only a testament to love but also a protected and acknowledged commitment under the law. The legal landscape is evolving, and your awareness and advocacy contribute to a more inclusive and supportive environment for trans couples seeking the recognition they deserve.

Navigating Name Changes and Gender Marker Updates

Navigating name changes and gender marker updates is a significant aspect of the wedding planning journey for many trans individuals. This process involves legal considerations that impact identification documents, and it's crucial to approach it with a clear understanding of the steps involved and the potential challenges that may arise.

For those who have not yet legally changed their names, the decision to do so can be a personal and empowering choice. It's important to research the requirements and procedures for name changes in your jurisdiction, as they can vary. Many places require the filing of a petition with the court, providing documentation such as a marriage certificate, and attending a court hearing. While the process can be straightforward, it's advisable to seek legal guidance to navigate any potential complications and ensure a smooth transition.

In the case of trans individuals who have already legally changed their names, the wedding may be an opportunity to update identification documents to reflect their affirmed names. Marriage certificates serve as a crucial document in this process, facilitating updates to other identification pieces such as driver's licenses, passports, and social security records. Keep in mind that requirements for updating these documents can vary by jurisdiction, and some may have additional steps or waiting periods.

Gender marker updates on identification documents are another consideration for trans individuals. While progress has been made in recognizing and accommodating gender diversity, not all jurisdictions have streamlined the process for updating gender markers. Some places may require proof of gender confirmation surgery or a court order, while others may have more inclusive policies.

Trans couples planning to marry should research the specific requirements for updating gender markers on identification documents in their jurisdiction. It may be helpful to contact the relevant government agencies or consult with legal professionals who specialize in LGBTQ+ rights for guidance on the steps involved.

In navigating name changes and gender marker updates, communication is key. Discuss your plans with your partner and ensure that you both have a clear understanding of the legal processes involved. Additionally, keeping open lines of communication with legal professionals, government agencies, and LGBTQ+ advocacy organizations can provide valuable insights and support.

Challenges may arise, particularly in jurisdictions where legal frameworks are less accommodating or inclusive. Discriminatory practices may manifest during the name change or gender marker update process. It's important to be aware of your rights, seek support from LGBTQ+ advocacy organizations, and, when necessary, consider legal recourse to address discriminatory practices.

Remember that the legal landscape is continually evolving, and progress is being made to create more inclusive and respectful procedures for name changes and gender marker updates. As you navigate these processes, celebrate the strides that have been made and contribute to advocacy efforts for continued positive change. Your journey towards updating identification documents is not just a legal formality; it's a meaningful step towards ensuring that your identity is affirmed and respected in all aspects of your life, including your marriage.

Addressing Legal Challenges and Advocacy

Addressing legal challenges and engaging in advocacy is an integral part of the journey for trans individuals navigating the complexities of marriage laws. While significant progress has been made in recognizing and respecting diverse gender identities, challenges may still arise, and advocating for inclusive and equitable legal practices becomes crucial.

Legal challenges can manifest in various forms, from outdated language in marriage laws to discriminatory practices when seeking a marriage license or updating identification documents. One common challenge is the presence of gendered language that may not fully encompass the diversity of gender identities. Advocacy efforts often focus on urging lawmakers to revise and modernize language in marriage laws to be inclusive and reflective of the LGBTQ+ community.

Trans individuals may also encounter obstacles when updating identification documents, particularly in jurisdictions where legal frameworks have yet to catch up with the evolving understanding of gender identity. Some places may still require proof of gender confirmation surgery or other medical procedures for gender marker updates, which can pose challenges for those who may not pursue or desire such procedures.

In the face of legal challenges, engaging in advocacy becomes a powerful tool for change. Many trans individuals and LGBTQ+ advocacy organizations work tirelessly to promote inclusivity and challenge discriminatory practices. If you encounter obstacles in the legal processes related to marriage, consider reaching out to these organizations for support and guidance.

Legal challenges may vary widely based on geographic location, as laws and regulations surrounding marriage and gender identity can differ significantly. Seeking legal advice from professionals who specialize in LGBTQ+ rights is essential. These legal experts can provide personalized guidance based on the specific laws and practices in your jurisdiction, helping you navigate challenges and advocating for your rights.

Engaging in advocacy extends beyond individual legal challenges. It involves contributing to broader efforts aimed at creating systemic change. This can include supporting legislative initiatives that promote inclusivity, participating in awareness campaigns, and sharing personal experiences to raise awareness about the unique challenges faced by trans individuals in the context of marriage.

Advocacy also plays a crucial role in challenging discriminatory practices and ensuring that trans individuals are treated with dignity and respect throughout the legal processes related to marriage. By sharing your experiences, whether positive or challenging, you contribute to a growing body of narratives that shed light on the need for more inclusive and equitable legal frameworks.

Participating in advocacy efforts may involve joining or supporting LGBTQ+ rights organizations, attending community events, or even sharing your story with lawmakers. It's a collective effort that not only benefits individuals navigating legal challenges but also contributes to creating a more inclusive and affirming environment for the entire LGBTQ+ community.

As you address legal challenges and engage in advocacy, remember that you are not alone. The LGBTQ+ community is resilient and has a rich history of advocacy that has paved the way for positive change. Your journey contributes to this ongoing legacy, and your efforts, no matter how small, contribute to building a more just and inclusive society for future generations.

Resources for Legal Support and Information

In the pursuit of navigating legal aspects related to marriage, trans individuals can find support and information through various resources that cater specifically to LGBTQ+ rights. Understanding your rights, seeking legal advice, and accessing resources can empower you to navigate the legal landscape with confidence and resilience.

Legal support for trans individuals often begins with LGBTQ+ legal organizations that specialize in advocating for the rights of the community. These organizations typically have legal professionals who are well-versed in the unique challenges faced by trans individuals, including those related to marriage laws, name changes, and gender marker updates.

One such resource is Lambda Legal, a national organization that focuses on LGBTQ+ civil rights. Lambda Legal offers legal support and advocacy, providing information on a range of issues affecting the LGBTQ+ community, including marriage, discrimination, and identity documentation. Their website is a valuable repository of legal resources, publications, and updates that can inform and empower individuals navigating the legal landscape.

The National Center for Lesbian Rights (NCLR) is another organization dedicated to advancing the rights of LGBTQ+ individuals. NCLR provides legal assistance and resources, covering a wide array of issues, including family and relationships, immigration, and transgender rights. Their team of legal experts works to ensure that the legal system is fair and inclusive for everyone.

For those seeking information specifically on transgender legal issues, the Transgender Legal Defense and Education Fund (TLDEF) is a valuable resource. TLDEF is committed to ending discrimination based on gender identity and expression. They provide legal resources, assistance with name changes, and information on navigating legal challenges related to transgender rights.

The American Civil Liberties Union (ACLU) has a longstanding commitment to defending the civil liberties of all individuals, including those in the LGBTQ+ community. Their LGBTQ+ Rights Project focuses on ensuring equal treatment under the law, and their website provides information on various legal issues, offering resources and updates.

Local LGBTQ+ community centers and organizations can also be excellent resources for legal support and information. Many cities have LGBTQ+ community centers that offer programs and services tailored to the needs of the community. These centers may provide information on local laws, legal clinics, or referrals to legal professionals with expertise in LGBTQ+ rights.

Legal professionals who specialize in LGBTQ+ rights can offer personalized guidance and support. When seeking legal advice, consider reaching out to attorneys or law firms with experience in transgender legal issues. They can provide insights into the specific laws and regulations in your jurisdiction and help you navigate any legal challenges you may encounter.

Online forums and communities where individuals share their experiences can be valuable sources of information. While not a substitute for legal advice, engaging with these communities can provide insights, perspectives, and emotional support. Platforms like Reddit may have subreddits dedicated to transgender issues, where community members share experiences and offer guidance.

Remember that knowledge is a powerful tool, and staying informed about your rights and legal options is essential. Whether you're planning a wedding, navigating name changes, or addressing legal challenges, accessing resources that cater specifically to LGBTQ+ rights can be instrumental in ensuring that your journey is informed, empowered, and supported. The legal landscape is evolving, and these resources are here to help you navigate it with confidence and resilience.

Preparing a Comprehensive Wedding Documentation Checklist

Preparing a comprehensive wedding documentation checklist is a crucial step in ensuring that all legal and logistical aspects of your wedding are seamlessly managed. This checklist is a roadmap that will guide you through the necessary documentation, helping you navigate the legal landscape with ease and confidence.

Start by understanding the specific documentation requirements in your jurisdiction. Marriage laws can vary significantly, so familiarize yourself with the regulations governing weddings in the location where you plan to marry. This may include obtaining a marriage license, understanding the necessary identification documents, and adhering to any waiting periods or residency requirements.

Once you have a clear understanding of the legal requirements, create a checklist that outlines each step of the documentation process. Include categories such as personal identification, proof of residency, and any additional documents required by the local authorities. This checklist will serve as a handy reference point as you gather the necessary paperwork.

Consider any name changes or updates to gender markers that may be part of your wedding documentation process. If you plan to change your name, research the specific requirements for name changes in your jurisdiction. Similarly, if you wish to update your gender marker on identification documents, be aware of the regulations and processes involved.

Include a section for obtaining a marriage license. This typically involves submitting an application, providing proof of identity and age, and paying any associated fees. Check the validity period of the marriage license, as some jurisdictions may have specific timelines within which the wedding ceremony must take place after obtaining the license.

If you have previously legally changed your name, ensure that your identification documents reflect your affirmed name. This may involve updating your driver's license, passport, and any other relevant documents. Verify the specific requirements and procedures for updating each form of identification.

Consider any additional documentation that may be required for a trans-inclusive wedding. This could include documentation related to gender confirmation surgeries or medical procedures if updating gender markers on identification documents. Be aware of the specific requirements and consult with legal professionals if needed.

In addition to legal documentation, include any paperwork required by your chosen venue or vendors. Some venues may request insurance or liability waivers, while vendors may require contracts or agreements. Having a comprehensive checklist ensures that you address both legal and logistical documentation needs.

Utilize resources provided by LGBTQ+ legal organizations to stay informed about your rights and legal options. These organizations often offer guides and publications on marriage laws, name changes, and gender marker updates specific to the LGBTQ+ community. Incorporate information from these resources into your checklist to stay well-informed.

Keep a timeline in mind as you prepare your wedding documentation checklist. Some documents may have specific processing times or waiting periods. Plan accordingly to ensure that all documentation is in order well before the wedding day, minimizing any last-minute stress or complications.

Lastly, communicate openly with your partner throughout the documentation process. Discuss any decisions related to name changes or gender marker updates and ensure that you are both aligned on the necessary paperwork. Sharing the responsibility of gathering documentation can make the process more collaborative and supportive.

In conclusion, a comprehensive wedding documentation checklist is a valuable tool that empowers you to navigate the legal and logistical aspects of your wedding with confidence. By understanding the specific requirements, staying informed about your rights, and collaborating with your partner, you can ensure that your wedding documentation process is smooth, inclusive, and tailored to your unique needs.

Chapter 7: Intersectionality in Trans Weddings

Welcome to Chapter 7: Intersectionality in Trans Weddings. As we embark on this chapter, we delve into the intricate and multifaceted nature of trans weddings, recognizing that the experiences of individuals within the trans community are shaped by a spectrum of identities and lived realities. Intersectionality is the lens through which we explore the interconnected layers of gender identity, race, ethnicity, sexual orientation, disability, and other aspects that collectively shape the unique narratives of trans couples.

In the realm of wedding planning, acknowledging and embracing intersectionality is vital. Each person brings a rich tapestry of identities and experiences, and the celebration of love should reflect and honor this diversity. This chapter serves as a guide to navigating the intersectional aspects of trans weddings, offering insights into creating inclusive and culturally sensitive celebrations that resonate with the distinct backgrounds and identities of trans couples.

Intersectionality prompts us to recognize that the challenges and joys experienced by trans individuals are not homogenous but deeply influenced by the intersections of various social categories. By understanding and appreciating these intersections, we can foster a wedding environment that celebrates the richness of diversity within the trans community.

Throughout this chapter, we'll explore how intersectionality manifests in attire choices, family dynamics, cultural traditions, and more. We'll delve into the importance of creating spaces that accommodate various abilities and consider the impact of socioeconomic factors on wedding planning. Our aim is to provide guidance that goes beyond a one-size-fits-all approach, recognizing that the journey of each trans couple is uniquely nuanced.

Ultimately, this chapter is an invitation to celebrate the mosaic of identities that contribute to the beautiful tapestry of trans weddings. By embracing intersectionality, we not only honor the diverse experiences within the trans community but also contribute to a more inclusive and equitable wedding landscape. So, let's navigate this chapter together, exploring the vibrant interplay of identities and crafting weddings that authentically reflect the beauty of love in all its diverse forms.

Embracing Diversity Within the Trans Community

Embracing diversity within the trans community is an essential cornerstone of creating inclusive and meaningful weddings. As we explore this aspect, it's crucial to recognize that the trans community is incredibly diverse, encompassing individuals of various gender identities, ethnicities, races, cultural backgrounds, sexual orientations, abilities, and socioeconomic statuses.

One of the first steps in embracing diversity is to acknowledge the multitude of gender identities that exist within the trans community. Transgender, genderqueer, non-binary, genderfluid—these are just a few identities that people may embrace. Understanding and respecting each individual's self-identified gender is fundamental to creating an inclusive wedding environment. This recognition lays the foundation for a celebration that truly honors the diversity of gender experiences within the trans community.

Cultural diversity is another facet to embrace within the trans community. Wedding ceremonies often intertwine with cultural traditions that hold deep significance for individuals and their families. Trans couples may draw from a variety of cultural backgrounds, each with its unique customs and rituals. Recognizing and incorporating these elements into the wedding celebration not only pays homage to the richness of cultural diversity but also adds a profound layer of meaning to the ceremony.

Moreover, embracing diversity within the trans community extends to acknowledging and respecting the intersections of identities. For instance, a trans person's experience is shaped not only by their gender identity but also by their racial or ethnic background, sexual orientation, and ability status. By understanding these intersections, we can foster a wedding environment that is attentive to the nuanced experiences of individuals with diverse identities.

Creating an inclusive space also involves recognizing and validating the journeys of trans individuals from various socioeconomic backgrounds. Economic disparities can significantly impact access to resources, including those related to wedding planning. Understanding and addressing these disparities ensures that wedding celebrations are accessible and affirming for all, regardless of financial circumstances.

The language used throughout the wedding planning process is a powerful tool for embracing diversity. Inclusive and respectful language, free from assumptions and stereotypes, contributes to a welcoming environment. For example, using gender-neutral language when communicating with couples and guests helps create an atmosphere that respects diverse gender identities.

Accessibility is another vital aspect of embracing diversity. Wedding venues, services, and accommodations should be accessible to individuals with different abilities. This includes considerations for physical accessibility, sensory accommodations, and any other specific needs that may arise. Ensuring that the wedding space is inclusive and accommodating reinforces the commitment to embracing diversity within the trans community.

In essence, embracing diversity within the trans community is about creating a wedding environment that celebrates the myriad identities, experiences, and backgrounds that individuals bring to their unions. It involves recognizing the unique intersectionalities that shape each person's journey and weaving these into the fabric of the celebration. By doing so, we not only honor the diverse experiences within the trans community but also contribute to a wedding landscape that is genuinely inclusive, equitable, and respectful of the rich tapestry of human identity.

Intersecting Identities: Race, Culture, and Gender

In the tapestry of trans weddings, the interplay of identities, including race, culture, and gender, adds vibrant threads that contribute to the unique stories of each couple. Recognizing and embracing the intersections of these identities is essential for creating weddings that authentically reflect the diverse and rich experiences within the trans community.

The intersection of race, culture, and gender brings forth a mosaic of perspectives and traditions that shape the way individuals approach and celebrate their unions. Couples may draw inspiration from cultural customs and familial traditions, intertwining them with their gender identities to create ceremonies that are deeply meaningful and reflective of their unique journeys.

For trans individuals of color, the intersection of racial and gender identities adds layers of complexity to their experiences. Understanding and acknowledging the impact of systemic inequalities and discrimination is crucial for creating an inclusive and supportive wedding environment. It involves actively addressing racial disparities, amplifying diverse voices, and ensuring that wedding planning processes are free from biases and stereotypes.

Cultural traditions play a significant role in shaping wedding celebrations. Couples often weave elements of their cultural heritage into the fabric of their ceremonies, from traditional attire to specific rituals and ceremonies. Embracing these cultural expressions fosters a sense of connection to one's roots and creates a wedding celebration that is both personal and communal.

Moreover, the intersection of gender with race and culture may influence attire choices and expressions of identity. Cultural expectations and norms can impact the way individuals navigate and express their gender identities. Embracing this intersectionality involves creating a space where couples feel free to express their gender identities authentically while also honoring the cultural contexts that shape their experiences.

Intersectional identities also extend to the dynamics of family involvement in wedding planning. Family expectations, cultural norms, and gender roles within different communities can influence the level of support or challenges couples may encounter. Recognizing and navigating these dynamics requires open communication and an understanding of the diverse familial structures and cultural contexts that may shape the wedding planning journey.

As couples navigate the intersection of race, culture, and gender in their weddings, it's essential to approach these conversations with sensitivity and a commitment to fostering understanding. Celebrating diversity means actively learning about and appreciating the unique cultural and racial backgrounds of each partner, their families, and the communities they belong to.

Inclusive wedding planning involves collaborating with vendors who respect and honor diverse cultural practices. From photographers to caterers, having a team that is attuned to the nuances of cultural and racial diversity ensures that the wedding celebration is approached with sensitivity and respect.

Ultimately, embracing the intersecting identities of race, culture, and gender is an invitation to celebrate the richness of human experiences within the trans community. It involves recognizing the interconnectedness of these identities and weaving them into the fabric of the wedding celebration. By doing so, couples create ceremonies that resonate with authenticity, honor their diverse backgrounds, and contribute to a more inclusive understanding of love and union.

Celebrating Love Across Different Abilities

Celebrating love across different abilities is a cornerstone of creating inclusive and accessible trans weddings. The diversity of abilities within the trans community adds unique dimensions to the wedding planning journey. By recognizing and embracing these differences, couples can ensure that their celebrations are not only joyous but also considerate of the varied needs and experiences of all attendees.

One crucial aspect of celebrating love across different abilities is creating a physically accessible wedding space. Considerations should be made for individuals with mobility challenges, ensuring that venues are equipped with ramps, elevators, and accessible restrooms. Outdoor venues should have smooth and navigable paths, allowing everyone to move freely and participate fully in the celebration.

Moreover, sensory accommodations are essential for individuals with diverse abilities. This may include providing quiet spaces for those who may be sensitive to noise, incorporating sign language interpreters for deaf or hard-of-hearing guests, or ensuring that lighting is adjustable to accommodate different visual needs. By proactively addressing these considerations, couples can create an environment where all attendees feel welcome and comfortable.

The celebration of love also involves accommodating various communication styles. Some guests may use alternative communication methods such as text or written notes, while others may benefit from visual aids or accessible materials. Couples can work with their vendors to provide information and communication in multiple formats, ensuring that everyone can engage and participate in the festivities.

The attire choices for the wedding party and guests should be flexible to accommodate different abilities. Some individuals may have specific clothing requirements based on mobility aids or sensory preferences. Working with inclusive and adaptive fashion designers can help ensure that everyone feels comfortable and stylish on the big day.

Family dynamics and traditions may also intersect with different abilities. Couples should engage in open and respectful conversations with their families to understand any specific considerations or needs related to accessibility. This proactive communication helps create an environment where everyone feels valued and included in the celebration.

Additionally, transportation considerations play a crucial role in celebrating love across different abilities. Ensuring that transportation options are accessible, whether it's arranging wheelchair-accessible vehicles or selecting venues with ample parking and drop-off points, contributes to the overall inclusivity of the event. This attention to detail reflects a commitment to making the wedding celebration accessible to all.

Inclusivity extends to the wedding ceremony itself, with couples considering how to make rituals and traditions accessible to individuals with diverse abilities. This may involve providing visual or tactile cues, incorporating assistive technology, or adapting rituals to be inclusive of various mobility levels. Working closely with celebrants or officiants who understand and respect the importance of accessibility is key.

Lastly, celebrating love across different abilities requires an attitude of openness and flexibility. Recognizing that everyone's needs and preferences may vary, couples can create an atmosphere where guests feel empowered to communicate their requirements. This collaborative approach fosters a sense of community and ensures that the celebration is a collective expression of love, joy, and inclusivity.

Ultimately, celebrating love across different abilities is about honoring the diversity of experiences within the trans community. By actively considering and addressing accessibility in wedding planning, couples create a celebration that reflects their commitment to inclusivity, allowing every guest to fully participate in and enjoy the joyous occasion. In doing so, they not only celebrate their love but also contribute to a more inclusive understanding of relationships and community.

Addressing Socioeconomic and Accessibility Challenges

Addressing socioeconomic and accessibility challenges in trans weddings is an integral aspect of creating celebrations that are not only joyous but also considerate of diverse circumstances and needs. Navigating these challenges involves recognizing the impact of economic disparities on wedding planning and ensuring that the wedding environment is accessible to individuals with varying financial circumstances and physical abilities.

Socioeconomic considerations play a significant role in the wedding planning journey. Couples may face challenges related to budget constraints, and the pressure to conform to traditional wedding norms can exacerbate these financial concerns. Addressing these challenges involves fostering open communication between partners about budget expectations, prioritizing essential elements, and exploring creative and cost-effective alternatives for various aspects of the wedding.

Recognizing that not all couples have the same financial resources, the wedding industry has seen a rise in the popularity of DIY (Do It Yourself) weddings and alternative, budget-friendly options. Couples can explore DIY decor, handmade invitations, and other personalized touches that not only reflect their uniqueness but also alleviate some of the financial burdens associated with traditional wedding expenses.

Moreover, addressing socioeconomic challenges involves seeking out vendors who are sensitive to various budget constraints. From photographers to caterers, vendors who offer a range of packages and are willing to work within different financial parameters contribute to a more inclusive and accessible wedding landscape. This collaborative approach ensures that couples can access quality services without compromising on their financial well-being.

Accessibility challenges, both physical and financial, also require careful consideration. Wedding venues should be chosen with accessibility in mind, ensuring that individuals with different physical abilities can navigate the space comfortably. Couples may opt for venues with accessible entrances, ramps, and other amenities that accommodate a range of needs. Additionally, selecting transportation options that are affordable and inclusive further addresses accessibility challenges.

Inclusivity in the face of socioeconomic challenges involves reimagining traditional wedding expectations. Couples can opt for intimate gatherings, daytime celebrations, or off-peak wedding dates, which may contribute to cost savings. The emphasis shifts from conforming to societal expectations to creating a celebration that is authentic, meaningful, and aligned with the couple's values and financial realities.

Community support plays a crucial role in addressing both socioeconomic and accessibility challenges. Friends and family who are willing to contribute time, skills, or resources can alleviate some of the burdens associated with wedding planning. Whether it's a friend offering photography services, a family member creating handmade decorations, or a loved one assisting with logistics, a collaborative and supportive community strengthens the foundation of the wedding celebration.

Addressing accessibility challenges also involves considering the needs of guests with diverse abilities. Couples can proactively communicate about accessible features of the venue, provide seating options for individuals with mobility challenges, and ensure that the ceremony and reception spaces are navigable for everyone. By anticipating and addressing these considerations, couples create a wedding environment that is welcoming to all attendees.

In essence, addressing socioeconomic and accessibility challenges in trans weddings is about fostering a wedding landscape that is both inclusive and considerate of diverse circumstances. It involves navigating financial constraints with transparency and creativity, choosing vendors who prioritize accessibility, and creating an environment where everyone, regardless of their abilities or economic status, can partake in the celebration. By doing so, couples contribute to a wedding culture that is not only beautiful but also socially conscious and welcoming to all.

Chapter 8: Honeymoon Bliss: Planning the Perfect Getaway

Welcome to Chapter 8: Honeymoon Bliss – Planning the Perfect Getaway. As you embark on this exciting chapter of your wedding journey, the focus shifts from wedding preparations to the anticipation of a romantic escape that marks the beginning of your shared life together. The honeymoon is a cherished time for couples to unwind, connect, and create memories that will last a lifetime.

In this chapter, we'll explore the ins and outs of planning a honeymoon that reflects your unique desires and celebrates the love you've pledged to each other. From choosing the ideal destination to crafting an itinerary that aligns with your interests, we'll guide you through the process of curating a getaway that sets the stage for a lifetime of shared adventures.

Whether you dream of basking in the sun on a tropical beach, exploring vibrant cities, or immersing yourselves in the serenity of nature, your honeymoon is an opportunity to tailor an experience that resonates with your personalities and aspirations. We'll delve into considerations such as budgeting, travel logistics, and activities that cater to both partners, ensuring that your honeymoon is not only blissful but also a harmonious beginning to your married life.

Beyond the practicalities, we'll explore the significance of the honeymoon as a time for relaxation, intimacy, and reflection on the beautiful journey you've embarked upon. From romantic dinners under the stars to adventurous excursions that strengthen your bond, the possibilities are as diverse as the love you share.

So, join us as we navigate the exciting terrain of honeymoon planning. Whether you're envisioning a tranquil escape to a secluded paradise or an exploration of bustling cityscapes, this chapter is designed to inspire and guide you in creating a honeymoon that becomes the first of many shared adventures in the remarkable tapestry of your married life. Let the journey to your perfect post-wedding retreat begin!

Selecting Trans-Inclusive Travel Destinations

Selecting trans-inclusive travel destinations for your honeymoon is a crucial step in ensuring that your post-wedding getaway is not only memorable but also supportive of your identities and experiences. As you dream about the perfect destination, consider places that go beyond just picturesque landscapes and luxurious accommodations – seek out locations that embrace diversity and foster an inclusive atmosphere for all travelers.

Start by researching destinations that have a reputation for LGBTQ+ friendliness and trans inclusivity. Look for places where local laws protect against discrimination based on gender identity and sexual orientation. Numerous travel guides and online resources offer valuable insights into the LGBTQ+ friendliness of different regions, helping you make an informed decision.

Consider the overall culture and attitudes of the destination towards gender diversity. Seek out places with a thriving LGBTQ+ community and visible support for gender inclusivity. Cities and regions known for hosting pride events, LGBTQ+ celebrations, and trans-focused initiatives are likely to provide a more welcoming environment for your honeymoon.

Look into the policies and practices of accommodations, restaurants, and activities in the destination. Choose hotels and resorts that have clear anti-discrimination policies and a track record of welcoming LGBTQ+ guests. Explore dining options that not only offer delicious cuisine but also prioritize inclusivity in their service and atmosphere.

When it comes to activities, consider those that align with your interests and values. Destinations that offer a range of inclusive experiences, from cultural tours to outdoor adventures, provide opportunities for you to celebrate your love while exploring the richness of the local community.

If you have specific interests or hobbies, such as art, music, or outdoor activities, look for destinations that cater to those passions while also being known for their LGBTQ+ inclusivity. Whether it's enjoying a vibrant arts scene, attending LGBTQ+ events, or exploring nature together, selecting a destination that aligns with your shared interests enhances the overall honeymoon experience.

Engage with the local LGBTQ+ community and trans support organizations in the destination. Connect with individuals who can provide firsthand insights into the inclusivity of the area and recommend LGBTQ+-friendly establishments. These connections can not only enhance your travel experience but also contribute to a sense of community during your honeymoon.

While planning, consider the accessibility of the destination for trans individuals. Think about factors such as healthcare facilities, gender-neutral restrooms, and the overall safety of trans individuals in public spaces. Choosing a destination that prioritizes these aspects ensures a more comfortable and stress-free honeymoon experience.

Lastly, don't hesitate to reach out to travel agencies or consultants specializing in LGBTQ+ travel. These experts can provide personalized recommendations based on your preferences and ensure that every aspect of your trip is tailored to your needs.

In the end, selecting trans-inclusive travel destinations for your honeymoon is about creating a space where you and your partner can fully enjoy each other's company without the worry of discrimination or discomfort. By intentionally choosing a destination that celebrates diversity and inclusivity, you set the stage for a honeymoon that not only showcases the beauty of the world but also honors the beauty of your love.

Travel Tips and Safety Considerations

Navigating travel tips and safety considerations for your honeymoon is a vital aspect of ensuring a smooth and enjoyable experience. Whether you're jetting off to a bustling city, a tranquil beach, or a remote mountain retreat, thoughtful planning can make all the difference in creating cherished memories while prioritizing your well-being.

First and foremost, research the local laws and regulations of your chosen destination, particularly those related to LGBTQ+ rights and gender identity. Understanding the legal landscape provides insight into potential challenges and helps you make informed decisions about your activities and interactions. Familiarize yourself with the local culture and customs, respecting the nuances that may shape the reception of LGBTQ+ individuals.

When it comes to accommodations, communication is key. Reach out to hotels and resorts in advance to inquire about their LGBTQ+ inclusivity and trans-friendly policies. Ask about their experience hosting LGBTQ+ guests and any specific amenities or considerations they offer. Establishing a rapport with your accommodations sets the tone for a welcoming and supportive environment during your stay.

Consider the timing of your honeymoon in relation to local events and festivals. Some destinations host LGBTQ+ pride celebrations or events that can enhance your experience and connect you with the local LGBTQ+ community. Conversely, being aware of potential challenges, such as political or social unrest, allows you to plan accordingly and prioritize your safety.

When packing for your honeymoon, think about the climate and the activities you have planned. Ensure you have appropriate clothing for various occasions, taking into account any cultural or modesty considerations. Pack essentials such as medications, important documents, and any necessary gender-affirming items. It's also advisable to carry a copy of important documents, such as passports and identification, in case of loss or theft.

Safety considerations extend beyond physical well-being to mental and emotional well-being as well.

Be mindful of your comfort level with public displays of affection and assess the local attitudes towards LGBTQ+ couples. While many destinations are inclusive and accepting, it's essential to gauge the cultural context and adapt your behavior accordingly to ensure a positive and stress-free experience.

Stay connected during your honeymoon by sharing your itinerary and accommodation details with trusted friends or family. Having a support network aware of your whereabouts can provide an added layer of security. Additionally, familiarize yourself with local emergency contact information and healthcare facilities. Knowing where to seek assistance in case of an emergency contributes to a sense of preparedness and confidence.

Utilize technology to your advantage by researching LGBTQ+ travel apps and resources that offer insights into safe spaces, LGBTQ+ friendly establishments, and local support networks. These tools can be invaluable for finding welcoming environments and connecting with like-minded individuals during your travels.

Lastly, trust your instincts and prioritize open communication with your partner. Discuss any concerns or anxieties you may have about safety or cultural differences. Establishing a shared understanding allows you to navigate potential challenges together and ensures that your honeymoon is a time of joy, connection, and mutual support.

In summary, travel tips and safety considerations are essential components of planning a honeymoon that is both enjoyable and secure. By being proactive, informed, and communicative, you set the stage for a honeymoon experience that not only celebrates your love but also respects and prioritizes your well-being as a trans couple.

Incorporating Honeymoon Plans into Wedding Budgets

Incorporating honeymoon plans into your wedding budget is a thoughtful and strategic approach to ensure that your post-wedding getaway aligns with your financial goals and priorities. While the allure of a dream honeymoon is undeniable, balancing the desire for an unforgettable experience with financial responsibility is key to setting the foundation for a harmonious start to your married life.

Begin by viewing your honeymoon as an integral part of the overall wedding experience. Instead of treating it as a separate expense, consider it a component of your wedding budget. This mindset shift allows you to allocate resources effectively and make informed decisions that reflect your values and priorities as a couple.

When crafting your wedding budget, set aside a specific amount for your honeymoon. This dedicated fund can be determined based on your financial capacity, taking into account your overall wedding expenses and any financial contributions from family members or loved ones. Establishing a clear budget for your honeymoon provides a financial framework that guides your planning decisions.

Prioritize your honeymoon expenses based on what matters most to you as a couple. Identify key elements such as accommodation, travel, activities, and meals that align with your vision for the perfect post-wedding retreat. Allocating budget categories allows you to distribute funds according to your preferences while maintaining financial discipline.

Consider alternative honeymoon options that align with your budget. Instead of viewing budget constraints as limitations, see them as opportunities to explore creative and meaningful alternatives. This could involve choosing a closer destination, opting for off-peak travel dates, or exploring cost-effective accommodations. By embracing flexibility and creativity, you can design a honeymoon experience that is both affordable and memorable.

Explore the potential for honeymoon contributions from loved ones. Instead of traditional wedding gifts, some couples choose to invite friends and family to contribute to their honeymoon fund.

Online platforms make it easy to set up a dedicated honeymoon registry where guests can contribute funds toward specific experiences or aspects of your getaway. This not only enhances your honeymoon budget but also allows loved ones to contribute to a meaningful and shared experience.

Stay mindful of hidden costs when planning your honeymoon. While certain expenses may be accounted for in your initial budget, unexpected costs can arise. Factor in potential contingencies or extra expenses to avoid financial stress during your trip. Planning for contingencies demonstrates financial foresight and ensures that you can navigate unforeseen circumstances without compromising your enjoyment.

Regularly review and adjust your honeymoon budget as needed. Wedding planning is a dynamic process, and adjustments may be necessary as circumstances change. Keep an open line of communication with your partner and revisit your budget periodically to ensure that it remains realistic and aligned with your financial goals.

Ultimately, incorporating honeymoon plans into your wedding budget is about striking a balance between creating cherished memories and financial responsibility. By thoughtfully considering your priorities, embracing creativity, and maintaining open communication, you can embark on a honeymoon that not only celebrates your love but also sets a positive tone for your financial journey as a married couple.

Trans-Friendly Accommodations and Services

Securing trans-friendly accommodations and services for your honeymoon is an essential aspect of ensuring that your travel experience is not only enjoyable but also respectful of your identities. As a trans couple, seeking out welcoming and inclusive spaces contributes to a sense of safety and comfort during your post-wedding retreat.

When researching accommodations, look for hotels, resorts, or vacation rentals that explicitly state their commitment to LGBTQ+ inclusivity. Many establishments now include information on their websites about their dedication to providing safe and welcoming spaces for all guests, regardless of gender identity or sexual orientation. This transparency is a positive indicator of an inclusive environment.

Consider reaching out directly to potential accommodations to inquire about their trans-friendly policies and practices. Communicating with the staff allows you to gain insights into their level of awareness and sensitivity to the unique needs of trans guests. Establishing this connection before your arrival fosters a sense of assurance that your stay will be respectful and accommodating.

Look for accommodations that offer gender-neutral facilities or restrooms. The presence of gender-neutral options demonstrates a commitment to inclusivity and recognizes the diverse identities of guests. This consideration extends beyond the physical facilities to the overall atmosphere, signaling that the establishment values the comfort and dignity of all individuals.

Explore reviews and testimonials from other LGBTQ+ travelers who have stayed at the accommodations you're considering. Online platforms and review websites often provide valuable insights into the experiences of fellow travelers, allowing you to gauge the trans-friendliness of a particular establishment. Positive reviews from trans individuals can be particularly reassuring.

In addition to accommodations, seek out trans-friendly services and amenities in the surrounding area. Restaurants, cafes, and entertainment venues that prioritize inclusivity contribute to a more seamless and enjoyable travel experience. Local businesses that display LGBTQ+ pride symbols or explicitly state their commitment to diversity are likely to be supportive spaces for trans individuals.

Take advantage of LGBTQ+ travel resources and apps that provide information about trans-friendly accommodations and services. These tools offer curated lists of establishments that have been vetted for their commitment to inclusivity. Utilizing such resources enhances your ability to make informed decisions and ensures that you have a range of welcoming options to choose from.

Consider the destination's overall reputation for LGBTQ+ inclusivity. Some cities and regions are renowned for their vibrant LGBTQ+ communities and welcoming atmospheres. Researching the cultural attitudes and legal protections in the area can provide insights into the overall climate for trans individuals, helping you make informed decisions about your travel plans.

Engage with LGBTQ+ travel communities and forums to seek recommendations from other trans travelers. Online platforms and social media groups dedicated to LGBTQ+ travel offer a wealth of firsthand experiences and insights. Connecting with individuals who share similar identities and travel preferences can provide valuable recommendations and enhance your overall travel experience.

In summary, securing trans-friendly accommodations and services for your honeymoon involves intentional research, open communication, and a proactive approach to ensuring that your travel experience aligns with your identities. By selecting establishments and services that prioritize inclusivity, you contribute to a travel landscape that respects and celebrates the diversity of all individuals, creating a honeymoon that is not only enjoyable but also affirming of your shared journey as a trans couple.

Building Lasting Memories: Honeymoon Experiences for Trans Couples

Building lasting memories during your honeymoon as a trans couple involves embracing experiences that reflect your unique identities and deepen the connection you share. From intimate moments to adventurous excursions, crafting a honeymoon filled with meaningful experiences sets the stage for a lifetime of cherished memories.

Begin by discussing your shared interests and preferences as a couple. What activities bring you joy and fulfillment? Whether it's exploring nature, immersing yourselves in local culture, or simply relaxing in each other's company, identifying common interests lays the foundation for a honeymoon that resonates with both partners.

Explore activities that align with your identities and celebrate your love. For instance, if you share a passion for the arts, consider attending local performances, art exhibits, or cultural events that showcase LGBTQ+ narratives. Seek out experiences that not only entertain but also affirm and reflect the richness of your relationship.

Plan moments of relaxation and intimacy that allow you to connect on a deeper level. Whether it's a private beach picnic, a spa day, or a quiet evening under the stars, prioritizing downtime amidst the excitement of your honeymoon creates space for reflection, conversation, and the cultivation of shared memories.

Engage with the local LGBTQ+ community and events in your chosen destination. Attend pride celebrations, LGBTQ+ gatherings, or community initiatives that allow you to connect with like-minded individuals. Building connections with the local LGBTQ+ community can enhance your honeymoon experience and create lasting friendships.

Consider incorporating gender-affirming experiences into your itinerary. This could involve activities such as shopping for gender-affirming clothing, seeking out LGBTQ+ inclusive spaces, or participating in events that celebrate gender diversity. Embracing these experiences contributes to a sense of empowerment and affirmation during your travels.

Capture your journey through creative means, whether it's through photography, journaling, or other forms of expression. Documenting your experiences allows you to relive the special moments of your honeymoon and create a tangible record of the love and joy you shared. Consider creating a scrapbook or digital album to preserve these memories for years to come.

Be open to spontaneity and unexpected adventures. While planning is essential, leaving room for serendipitous moments adds an element of surprise and excitement to your honeymoon. Whether it's stumbling upon a hidden gem, trying a new activity, or exploring off-the-beaten-path locations, embracing spontaneity enhances the richness of your travel experience.

Celebrate milestones and anniversaries during your honeymoon. If your trip coincides with a significant date, such as the anniversary of your first date or the day you got engaged, take the opportunity to commemorate these moments. Whether it's a special dinner, a romantic gesture, or a heartfelt exchange of vows, marking milestones during your honeymoon adds layers of meaning to your shared journey.

Engage in conversations about your future together and the adventures you envision. Use this time to dream, plan, and set intentions for the years ahead. Whether it's discussing future travel plans, career aspirations, or personal goals, these conversations deepen your connection and build a foundation for the life you're creating as a married couple.

In summary, building lasting memories during your honeymoon as a trans couple involves intentional planning, shared experiences, and a commitment to celebrating your unique journey. By embracing activities that resonate with your identities, prioritizing intimate moments, and capturing the essence of your love, you create a honeymoon that not only marks the beginning of your married life but also sets the stage for a lifetime of meaningful adventures together.

Chapter 9: DIY Trans-Inclusive Weddings: Crafting Your Perfect Day

Welcome to Chapter 9: DIY Trans-Inclusive Weddings – a guide to crafting your perfect day with intention, creativity, and authenticity. In this chapter, we'll explore the empowering world of Do-It-Yourself (DIY) weddings, tailored specifically to celebrate the love and uniqueness of trans couples.

Planning your wedding is a deeply personal and meaningful journey, and DIY weddings provide an incredible opportunity to infuse every aspect of your celebration with your personalities, preferences, and shared experiences. This chapter is designed to inspire and guide you through the process of creating a trans-inclusive wedding that reflects your love story and values.

Embarking on the DIY route allows you to take control of your wedding planning, ensuring that every detail aligns with your vision for a day that is not only trans-affirming but also a true representation of your authentic selves. From personalized decor to inclusive ceremony rituals, we'll delve into the creative possibilities that DIY weddings offer.

As you navigate through this chapter, you'll discover practical tips, creative ideas, and heartfelt advice on how to design a wedding that goes beyond societal norms and embraces the diversity of your love. Whether you're envisioning a small and intimate gathering or a grand celebration, the principles of DIY trans-inclusive weddings can be adapted to suit your unique desires and preferences.

Remember, your wedding day is a canvas waiting to be painted with the colors of your love, identity, and shared dreams. So, let's dive into the world of DIY Trans-Inclusive Weddings, where creativity knows no bounds, and every detail becomes a brushstroke in the masterpiece of your perfect day. Get ready to embark on a journey of self-expression, celebration, and love as you craft a wedding that is distinctly and beautifully yours.

Embracing the DIY Spirit in Wedding Planning

Embracing the DIY spirit in wedding planning is a transformative journey that goes beyond mere tasks—it's about infusing your celebration with authenticity, creativity, and the unique essence of your love story. As a trans couple, the DIY approach allows you to break free from traditional constraints and craft a wedding experience that resonates with your identities and celebrates the beauty of your connection.

At its core, embracing the DIY spirit means taking an active role in shaping every facet of your wedding day. It's an invitation to become the architects of your celebration, infusing it with the values, symbols, and representations that matter most to you. This journey begins by acknowledging that your wedding is not just an event but a profound expression of your identities and the journey you've undertaken together.

One of the empowering aspects of DIY wedding planning is reclaiming agency over your narrative. Trans individuals often face challenges when it comes to societal expectations and norms. The DIY approach allows you to challenge these norms and redefine what a wedding should look like. Whether it's through personalized vows, unique ceremony rituals, or unconventional attire choices, each decision becomes a deliberate act of self-expression.

The process of embracing the DIY spirit encourages collaboration and shared creativity between partners. It's an opportunity to discuss, dream, and co-create a celebration that reflects both of your personalities. By engaging in this collaborative effort, you strengthen the foundation of your partnership and create a wedding that is a true representation of the love you share.

DIY weddings are also an ode to resourcefulness and sustainability. Repurposing, upcycling, and creating elements by hand not only infuse your wedding with character but also contribute to a more eco-friendly celebration. This sustainable approach aligns with the values of many couples who wish to minimize their environmental impact while crafting a celebration that is uniquely theirs.

Moreover, the DIY spirit in wedding planning provides a platform for telling your story authentically. Whether it's through handmade decorations, custom-designed invitations, or a personally curated playlist, each element becomes a chapter in the story of your love. This authenticity resonates with guests, creating a more intimate and meaningful experience for everyone involved.

It's essential to recognize that embracing the DIY spirit doesn't mean taking on every task alone. DIY weddings can still involve collaboration with friends, family, and even professionals for certain aspects. The key is to maintain a hands-on approach in shaping the details that matter most to you. This balance ensures that your wedding is both a communal effort and a deeply personal expression.

In conclusion, embracing the DIY spirit in wedding planning is a celebration of love, identity, and creativity. It's about taking control of your narrative, collaborating with your partner, and crafting a celebration that is a genuine reflection of your unique connection. So, let the DIY journey begin, and may every choice, every detail, and every moment speak volumes about the beauty of your trans-inclusive love story.

DIY Decor and Wedding Invitations

Designing DIY decor and wedding invitations is a delightful way to infuse your celebration with a personalized touch that reflects the uniqueness of your love story. In this section, we'll explore how crafting your own decorations and invitations allows you to express your identities, share your narrative, and create a warm and inviting atmosphere for your guests.

Let's begin with DIY decor. From the ceremony space to the reception venue, handmade decorations provide an opportunity to infuse your wedding with your personalities and aesthetic preferences. Consider creating custom signage that welcomes guests with a heartfelt message or designing centerpieces that incorporate elements significant to your journey as a couple. The possibilities are endless, and the act of crafting these details together can be a bonding experience for you and your partner.

When it comes to DIY wedding invitations, the process involves more than just selecting fonts and colors—it's a chance to tell your love story and set the tone for your celebration. Begin by brainstorming themes, symbols, or motifs that hold personal meaning for both of you. Incorporate these elements into the design to create invitations that feel authentically yours.

Consider crafting a narrative within your invitations. Share snippets of your story, such as how you met, your shared interests, or the significance of your chosen wedding date. This personal touch not only engages your guests but also invites them into the intimate world of your relationship. It's an opportunity to celebrate your journey and build anticipation for the joyous occasion.

Experiment with various materials to add texture and depth to your invitations. Whether it's incorporating handmade paper, fabric, or other tactile elements, these choices contribute to a sensory experience for your guests. The effort put into crafting each invitation becomes a tangible expression of the care and thoughtfulness you've invested in creating a unique celebration.

Include gender-inclusive language in your invitations to ensure that every guest feels welcome and acknowledged. Thoughtful language choices, such as using neutral terms like "wedding party" instead of gender-specific titles, contribute to a more inclusive and affirming atmosphere. This attention to detail aligns with the values of a trans-inclusive celebration.

Explore digital tools and platforms that allow you to design and print your invitations at home. DIY doesn't necessarily mean handcrafted from scratch; leveraging technology can simplify the process while still allowing you to customize every detail. Many online services offer templates and design tools that cater to various styles and preferences.

Engage in DIY workshops or enlist the help of artistic friends and family members. Whether it's calligraphy, illustration, or other creative skills, involving loved ones in the process adds a communal aspect to your wedding preparations. Collaborative efforts can lead to unique and beautiful results that reflect the shared love surrounding your union.

Remember, the essence of DIY decor and wedding invitations lies in the personal touch you bring to each element. It's an opportunity to celebrate your love authentically, share your story, and create an environment that resonates with both you and your guests. So, pick up those crafting materials, let your creativity flow, and watch as your wedding decorations and invitations become a testament to the beauty of your trans-inclusive love story.

Creating a Trans-Inclusive Wedding Website

Creating a trans-inclusive wedding website is a modern and considerate way to share essential information, celebrate your love story, and ensure that all your guests feel informed and welcome. In this section, we'll explore the elements that make a wedding website trans-inclusive and how this digital platform can serve as a central hub for communicating the details of your celebration.

Start by choosing a user-friendly platform that allows for easy customization. Many website builders offer intuitive interfaces with drag-and-drop features, making it accessible for couples with varying levels of technical expertise. Select a template that resonates with your style and provides ample space for the unique aspects of your trans-inclusive wedding.

Introduce yourselves on the website in a way that reflects your authentic identities. Share your pronouns, details about your journey as a couple, and any cultural or personal aspects that you'd like your guests to know. This not only sets the tone for an inclusive celebration but also helps guests connect with your narrative.

Include a section on your website that educates guests about gender-inclusive language and etiquette. This can be an informative and supportive resource for those who may be less familiar with terminology or practices related to gender diversity. Consider providing links to external resources for further exploration.

Create a dedicated space for your wedding party and include information about their roles, responsibilities, and pronouns. This is especially important for trans individuals who may have specific preferences regarding how they are addressed and acknowledged. Highlighting your wedding party's diversity contributes to a trans-inclusive atmosphere.

When outlining the schedule of events, be mindful of the timing and pacing of activities. Consider building in breaks or quiet moments to accommodate guests who may need additional time or space. This thoughtful approach ensures that everyone can fully participate in and enjoy each aspect of your celebration.

Offer multiple options for attire suggestions, emphasizing that guests should wear whatever makes them feel comfortable and affirmed. This flexibility is crucial for creating an inclusive environment, allowing guests to express their gender identities and styles authentically. Providing examples or mood boards can be helpful for those seeking guidance.

Include information about the venue's facilities and accessibility features. If applicable, mention the availability of gender-neutral restrooms and any other accommodations that contribute to a trans-friendly environment. This transparency helps guests feel more at ease and ensures they can navigate the celebration comfortably.

Provide a platform for guests to share their pronouns when RSVPing. This simple yet impactful addition allows you to address individuals using their correct pronouns and fosters a sense of respect and acknowledgment. Make it clear that providing pronouns is optional but encouraged.

Consider incorporating a digital guestbook or interactive features that allow guests to leave messages, well-wishes, or advice. This creates a virtual space for community-building and reinforces the sense of connection among your guests. Encourage them to share stories, memories, or expressions of support on the website.

In conclusion, creating a trans-inclusive wedding website is a powerful way to communicate essential information, celebrate your love authentically, and foster an atmosphere of respect and inclusion. By thoughtfully curating the content and features on your website, you contribute to a celebration that reflects the diverse identities and stories of all your guests. So, embark on this digital journey, infuse your website with the warmth of your love, and create a virtual space that sets the stage for a truly trans-inclusive wedding celebration.

Budget-Friendly DIY Tips for Trans Couples

Navigating wedding expenses can be a significant aspect of the planning process for any couple, and for trans couples embracing a DIY approach, there are plenty of budget-friendly tips to ensure your celebration is both meaningful and affordable.

Firstly, consider repurposing and upcycling materials for your DIY projects. From decor to centerpieces, utilizing items you already have or sourcing second-hand materials not only reduces costs but also contributes to a more sustainable and eco-friendly celebration. Get creative with your choices, as repurposing can add unique and personalized touches to your wedding elements.

Explore local and online resources for affordable DIY supplies. Many communities have craft stores, thrift shops, or online platforms where you can find budget-friendly materials for your projects. Engaging with local businesses not only supports the community but may also lead to discovering hidden gems and unique items that add character to your wedding decor.

Collaborate with friends and family who have artistic or crafting skills. DIY projects become even more enjoyable when shared with loved ones, and tapping into their expertise can be both cost-effective and strengthen the sense of community around your celebration. Whether it's crafting decorations, designing invitations, or assembling wedding favors, involving others fosters a collaborative and joyous atmosphere.

Consider DIY alternatives for traditional wedding elements that may come with a hefty price tag. For example, instead of purchasing a costly wedding cake, explore the option of a DIY dessert bar with homemade treats. This not only adds a personal touch but also allows for a diverse and budget-friendly spread that your guests will likely appreciate.

Optimize your budget by prioritizing DIY projects that align with your vision and values. Identify aspects of the wedding that are most important to you and your partner, and allocate your time and resources accordingly. By focusing on what truly matters to you, you can create a celebration that feels authentic and meaningful without breaking the bank.

Explore free or low-cost venues for your celebration. Public parks, community spaces, or even the backyard of a friend or family member can serve as beautiful and budget-friendly locations for your wedding. Choosing an affordable venue allows you to allocate more resources to DIY projects and personalized touches.

DIY your wedding favors to both save on costs and offer guests a thoughtful token of appreciation. From homemade candles to personalized treats, crafting your own wedding favors adds a touch of sincerity and creativity to your celebration. Choose favors that align with your theme or share a glimpse of your love story.

Consider a potluck-style catering approach, where guests contribute to the meal. This not only lowers catering costs but also allows for a diverse and personalized menu. Coordinate with guests to ensure a variety of dishes and accommodate dietary preferences, creating a shared and communal aspect to the dining experience.

Lastly, leverage online tutorials and resources for guidance and inspiration. From DIY wedding blogs to video tutorials, the internet is a treasure trove of ideas and instructions for budget-friendly projects. Use these resources to learn new skills, discover creative alternatives, and gain insights into making the most of your DIY wedding journey.

In summary, embracing a budget-friendly DIY approach as a trans couple involves resourcefulness, collaboration, and thoughtful prioritization. By repurposing materials, collaborating with loved ones, exploring affordable alternatives, and focusing on what truly matters to you, you can create a wedding celebration that is not only meaningful but also financially sustainable. Enjoy the process of crafting a celebration that reflects your love story while keeping a keen eye on your budget, ensuring that your wedding is as affordable as it is beautiful.

Conclusion: A Guide to Lasting Love and Authentic Celebrations

As we reach the conclusion of this guide, it's with heartfelt excitement and a deep sense of gratitude for sharing this journey with you. Navigating the intricacies of wedding planning, particularly for trans couples, is a unique adventure filled with creativity, resilience, and the celebration of authentic love. In this concluding section, we reflect on the guiding principles that have woven through each chapter, offering a tapestry of insights and inspiration to carry forward into your own wedding planning experience.

Our journey began with "Understanding Your Vision," encouraging you to define and embrace a wedding narrative that reflects your unique love story. From there, we delved into the intricacies of attire, family dynamics, vendor selection, and the rich tapestry of inclusive rituals. Each chapter was a step toward creating a celebration that honors your identities, values, and the profound commitment you share.

Throughout this guide, the power of authenticity emerged as a driving force. Whether it's in the choices you make for attire, the rituals you incorporate, or the relationships you cultivate, authenticity has been the North Star guiding you toward a celebration that is uniquely and unapologetically yours. We explored the beauty of DIY projects, budget-friendly tips, and the inspiring success stories within the trans community, showcasing the creativity and resilience that flourishes when love takes center stage.

In the spirit of community, this guide aimed to connect you with resources, ideas, and the collective wisdom of those who have walked this path before. Wedding planning is not merely a checklist of tasks; it's a journey of self-discovery, partnership, and the creation of lasting memories. As you move forward, may the insights shared in these chapters serve as companions, offering guidance, support, and a source of inspiration.

Remember, this is not just a guide to planning a wedding; it's a celebration of lasting love and authentic unions. The chapters may end, but your journey continues. As you step into the future, may your love story unfold with each passing day, a testament to the resilience, creativity, and unwavering authenticity that defines your unique bond. Cheers to your love, your celebration, and the beautiful chapters yet to be written in the book of your shared life.